The 10 Essential Habits of Sales Superstars

The 10 Essential Habits *of* Sales Superstars

Plugging into the Power of Ten

BUTCH BELLAH

© 2014 by Butch Bellah All rights reserved

Sales Power Publishing
1810 Commerce Street #1016
Dallas, TX 75201

ISBN 978-0-9904301-0-0 paperback
ISBN 978-0-9904301-1-7 ebook

Printed and bound in the United States of America.

All rights reserved. No part of this book may be reproduced, translated, stored in a retrieval system, or transmitted in any form, or by any means, electronic, mechanical, photocopying, or otherwise without written permission except in the case of brief quotations embodied in critical articles and reviews.

Library of Congress Control Number: 2014909259

The author photo (back cover and page 91) are courtesy of Photography by Misty.

ACKNOWLEDGMENTS

Like most books, there is no way this one would've seen the light of day had it not been for the support, encouragement, and love of so many people. This is definitely not a one-man show.

My thanks go to my family for past and present support. First and foremost, I want to thank my wife, Angie. She's been my best friend, high school sweetheart, and the love of my life for almost twenty-nine years. She believed in me at times when I didn't believe in myself and has always been my biggest fan and loudest cheerleader; I love you more than you'll ever know. To my three children: Jonathan (who designed my website), Whitney (who designed my book cover), and Sidney (who I believe will truly be a Difference Maker in the world), I love you all so much. You make me proud every single day, thank you for putting up with me being that Dad who was always standing in front of the crowd (even when it embarrassed you) instead of blending in. To my sister, Susan who is the glue that holds the family together and who always stood up for her little brother, thank you. I love ya!

To my mentor and friend for the past twenty-five years, Noble Feldman, your friendship, leadership, and willingness to share your knowledge has changed the course of my life. Thank you for your encouragement, support, and taking a chance on a twenty-one-year-old kid all those years ago.

To my fellow Sales Coach, Hugh Liddle, thank you. Thanks for talking me off the ledge in moments of discouragement, and being a sounding board for me. Your experience and shared desire to change the selling world is so inspirational.

To Will Broyles, Jim Broyles, and the entire Broyles families, thank you for your confidence in me and for your support of my passion to be a Difference Maker.

To my editor Terri Boekhoff, where would I be without you? Your knowledge, encouragement, and kicks in the pants kept this train on the track and proved invaluable. If people could only see what I started with and what you turned it into. Thank you so much.

There are three people who I wish could've been around to see the results—my late parents, Don and Maudie (Toot) Bellah and my late brother, Scott. I grew up with a Mama and Daddy who taught me at an early age to believe I could do anything. I was encouraged to be creative, to think and to ask questions. I know they'd both be so proud. And, my brother Scott, what a character. My best friend growing up (we were two years apart), he truly was the funniest person in the family. I miss the three of you every day.

For Don, Maudie, and Scott

TABLE OF CONTENTS

Introduction *1*

Preparing for Growth *7*

The Power of the Power of Ten *9*

Habit #1—Building the Base *13*

Habit #2—Developing Tomorrow's Sales *21*

Habit #3—Gaining an Extra Week Each Year *27*

Habit #4—Goals—Setting and Focusing on Them *33*

Habit #5—Getting Past the Gatekeeper and Getting on Their Calendar *39*

Habit #6—Keeping Your Current Clients Happy *47*

Habit #7—Preparing To Succeed *55*

Habit #8—Know Your Customer *65*

Habit #9—Keeping the Pipeline Full *69*

Habit #10—Never Stop Learning and Growing *75*

Epilogue *85*

Appendix—Tools for Creating the Habits of Sales Superstars *89*

About the Author *91*

Introduction

Whether you're new to the world of sales or a seasoned veteran, the book you're now reading can and will change your life. The information it contains is applicable to those who have been in business for five minutes or five decades. It requires no large investment in materials, software, or hardware. It is timeless, simple, and can be adapted for anyone in virtually any profession.

I want to introduce you to the ten habits that will transform your sales results. They, my friend, are perfect for you! In fact, this is the training you should've gotten when you started your job. Sadly, most of you didn't.

But, be warned; there is a huge difference between simple and easy! Developing these habits is simple; it is not easy. It takes a commitment from you—a commitment to buy in and put them into action. Unfortunately, this is where most people fail. They read about great sales techniques and hope that by osmosis they will somehow be absorbed into their being. It just doesn't work that way.

For more than twenty-five years, I've successfully used some or all of these habits. I've refined them, added to them, and finally assembled the ten you will read and learn about here. Each one of these ten is proven to work. They have been tested in real-world sales situations. They were developed and honed through in-person, face-to-face selling in the field—not from some ivory tower of sales management.

You should know that I've been where you are—on the front line of sales calls and managing sales teams. I've set appointments, done needs analyses, worked with clients, made presentations, and made lots of sales. I've been doing it for more than a quarter century in one form or another. I have plenty of real world experience to draw from.

The next thing you need to know about me is that on May 20, 2009 I had triple bypass heart surgery at forty-three-years old. So, what does my heart surgery have to do with you and your sales success? Well, if I would have been asked on May 18, 2009 if I wanted triple bypass heart surgery, I would've told you that I don't want it, don't need it, and can't afford it! Do those objections sound familiar?

Are you hearing any of those today?

Guess what? When the cardiologist showed me I had an artery with 70%, two with 80%, and one with a 90% blockage I changed my tune. Not only did I now need it, but I wanted it, didn't care about the cost, and wanted an expert doing it!

Unfortunately in today's business world, you have customers and potential customers out there whose business is in as critical a condition as my heart was. They have *blockage* and most don't know it! Many have no idea they need your help…*yet*. What they need is for you to be the expert—to be a *professional salesperson*!

Introduction

That is what this little book, *The Ten Essential Habits of Sales Superstars,* is all about—giving you the tools, techniques, and strategies to be the expert. When the surgeon walks into the operating room, he doesn't have to think about washing his hands first. He developed that habit long ago. Now he can concentrate on using his expertise as a surgeon.

Too many times, as salespeople, we find ourselves looking for a magic wand, some kind of secret or the next new idea. Newsflash: There are no new ideas—only good ideas that you are not using!

Let's face it, no matter what business you're in; whether you sell a tangible product or an intangible service—you have competition. Somebody else does what you do, and in many cases they'll do it cheaper.

If you're tired of losing business over price, *The Ten Essential Habits of Sales Superstars* can and will give you the competitive edge you've been seeking. Embrace it and put it to work in your life immediately—and you'll see immediate results. But remember, you cannot change your results until you change your habits. That's where this book comes in—when used properly and followed religiously, it will change your habits and your results. Period.

You're going to learn to develop ten proven habits—not 101, not seventy-five, but *ten* powerful changes in your behavior that will increase your sales, your income, and ultimately your happiness and satisfaction. You'll be more organized, more goal oriented, and know every moment of every day of every week of every month where you stand in relation to your goals and what you have to do to achieve them.

All you have to do is put these ten habits to work in your life and business. It's just that simple.

Perhaps the best part is that you can start today right where you are. What you are about to learn should become a part of what you do daily, weekly, monthly—for life. Remember, only you can effect change in your situation. Nobody can open your mind and dump knowledge and good practices into it without your consent. You must take the lead and take it seriously enough to learn and internalize these principles, strategies, and techniques.

As you read this book, you'll very likely say to yourself, "I knew that," or, "Well, that's simple enough," and you will be absolutely right. But, why aren't you doing these things? Knowing and doing are very different. If you *know* it and your competition is *doing* it who is going to be winning?

Does it sound like I am challenging you? Well, I am. Everything in this book has been done before. Everything. But, has it been done by *you*?

If not, you are in luck. You still have a chance to change the way you approach your job, your prospects, your customers, and your life. And, rest assured that if you'll make each of these ten habits part of the way you do business and live your life—you'll not only be a minimum of ten percent better than your competition, but you'll also have ten times more fun.

As a general rule salespeople tend to need immediate feedback. I know I do. I want to know if I'm doing good, bad, or otherwise. I need to see the score. Am I winning or losing? And what do I need to do to change that.

One of the great things about this book is that you get that immediate feedback. You get things you can do now! Every one of these suggested habits are designed for you to begin *today* and continue with every day. They are things you must make a habit

Introduction

of doing daily. You don't have to wait six weeks or six months to see benefits. You can see them *now*. In the Appendix on page 89, there are links to forms that you can download. Use these forms to jumpstart the creation of new habits.

But, you have to put them into practice because every potential customer that comes in contact with an untrained or poorly-trained salesperson is wasted. You should view them not only as a lost sale today, but forever; because most of them won't give your company or business a chance to earn their trust again.

You are truly better off not having that potential customer come in contact with your company at all. At least that way, they have a neutral feeling and not a negative one.

So, what do you do?

For one thing, you should never stop improving your skills. If you are a sales manager—you should constantly be working to grow, manage, and coach your team.

If you were to grade your sales team today, I'm sure you would have some "A" players, some "B" players, maybe some "C" players, and even a few "D" players. (Hopefully, you don't have any "F" players.) A good training program will keep the skills of your "A" players sharp and continue to let them grow personally (otherwise, you may very well lose them), and it will also move the others up a level.

For example, you should strive to add your "B" players to the "A" team, your "C" players to the "B" team, and so on. Never stop training. If you find that your sales team knows everything, try to find someone to buy your business—*quickly!*

The American Society for Training and Development (ASTD) reports that American businesses spent $130 billion or $1,068 per employee on learning and development in 2008—even with the problems in the economy. I know of some companies that actually committed more to training *because* of the economy.

Unfortunately, when business is great a lot of mistakes can be hidden and a lot of errors can be overcome. But, business is never good enough to stop training your sales team—no matter what.

Even the superstars take batting practice—and many times they're the first ones out and the last to leave. They didn't get to be superstars by accident.

Jack Welch suggests that you fire the bottom 10% of your employees (sales team) every year. While some may see that as a bit drastic, it may be necessary in today's world.

If you would replace the bottom 10% ("D" players) with just average performers, you would have gone a long way to improving your sales volume, customer service, and the customer's experience with your company.

This book will renew your focus on what it takes to grow your business. More importantly, you'll learn what I call The Golden Rule of The Power of Ten:

I do not have to be twice as good as my competition . . .
just 10% better.

Finally, there are no short cuts. Liking these ideas, agreeing with them, believing in them, and not doing them will get you nowhere. As Yoda would say, "Do or do not. There is no try."

Preparing for Growth

Before we begin, it's vitally important that you accept the fact you can do more and you deserve more. Nobody is perfect and your skills can be improved—but by far the most important part about this is your attitude. Are you ready to accept a better career and better life? Is your mind open to new ideas, new processes, and new procedures?

Let me share a story with you: Two fishermen are at a lake and one can't help but notice that the other always puts the big fish back in but keeps the little ones. This goes on for several hours. Curiosity got the better of him and he just had to ask, "Say, I see that you keep putting the big fish back but keeping the small ones. Can I ask you why?

"Oh, that's easy to answer, I only have a ten-inch frying pan. It's been in our family for generations!"

Pastor Joel Osteen asks, "How big is your frying pan?" Have you been conditioned to think you're only deserving of the little fish? Do you dare to think bigger? You're not going to see increase if you're stuck in old ways of thinking. Start believing that you deserve the biggest and the best.

Wow! What a powerful story. Whether you agree with all of Joel Osteen's ministry or not, the story is clear; we have all been conditioned to accept and even expect certain things—are we limiting ourselves? I think so.

What would and could we do if we didn't fear failure, rejection, embarrassment, or humiliation? What would we try—and therefore accomplish? We all need to increase the size of our frying pans. We need to expect bigger and better—for our expectations are usually met—whether good or bad.

What are you doing that is limiting your growth? Throw off those things that are weighing you down and reach, dream big, dream bold, but dream as if you *expect* those dreams to come true.

Think about what is holding you back, but don't dwell on it. That's the negative. Rather, focus on what can help you exceed your own expectations and limitations. It's not the economy, the government, your education, etc. Those have all been overcome by others. Don't fall into the trap of letting outside influences set your standards! Go for it!

Hopefully this book is the start of a much, much larger frying pan for you.

ಜ

**If you're as good as you're going to be,
life is as good as it's going to get.
~Butch Bellah**

The Power of the Power of Ten

Let's create a fictitious business or salesperson producing $750,000 a year in sales. For some of you that may be high—for other's it's probably extremely low. But, it will illustrate the point I want to make—$750,000 in sales. If you have a gross profit of 25%—again for your business that may or may not be applicable, but follow me here. Twenty-five percent gross profit would generate $187,500 each year in revenue.

Now, for the sake of this illustration, let's assume this business's expenses were 20% of sales. Twenty percent of $750,000 would give you $150,000 in expenses, which we need to subtract from the revenue.

So, the result of all this hard work is a bottom line of $37,500.

Now, I'm going to show you The Power of Ten. Let's plug in a sales increase of 10%—another $75,000 a year. Annual sales would now be $825,000.

Let's say we could increase gross profit by 10%. Not the dollars, but the percentage. Instead of 25% gross profit, let's say we could—through a lot of hard work, tough negotiation, and actual selling skills—make it 27.5% (we increased it 2.5% or 10% of the original gross profit of 25%). All of a sudden our revenue is $226,875 (instead of $187,500). Now you're talking!

But, what if we could reduce expenses by 10% (cut that 20% to 18%). Expenses for the year would be $148,500.

Look what we've done: We've taken the three main line items on our P&L and affected each of them by just 10%, but the results are staggering. Now, instead of putting $37,500 on the bottom line, we've increased that to $78,375.

Are you ready for this? That's an increase of 109%! That, my friends is The Power of Ten.

Okay. So, how do we do that? It's not easy. In fact, it takes something that a lot of people aren't willing to do—work!

I know what you're saying, "Well in my business if I increase sales there's no way I can increase gross profit, because it's all about price." Baloney! If you truly believe that, you are in for a tough time. Forget that garbage. Contrary to what even your customers will tell you, it is not all about price. And if you are selling simply on price, you are not a professional salesperson. Your company can hire someone for eight dollars an hour to go out and cut prices. It's not that difficult. You have to *sell*!

You could also just as easily substitute referrals, closing percentage, and order size for those three items and see the same kind of impact in your own personal P&L! If you can change just three aspects of your sales career by just 10%, you will see magnificent results—results you may have thought weren't possible. And it's all because of a slight 10% increase in a few areas of your business.

The Power of Ten is just that *powerful*!

So, are you ready? Are you committed to putting this to work? Are you willing to do even the things you think are unnecessary in order to see your sales life change?

The upper one half of 1% of all salespeople in the world use these ten essential habits (and probably a few others). Are you ready to begin your journey to join that group?

Are you ready to be the expert?

☯

The best time to plant a tree was twenty years ago. The next best time is now!
~Chinese Proverb

Building the Base

Habit #1
Make Ten New Contacts Weekly

In order to have any business at all, one must make contacts. Let me first give you the following definitions according to my internal dictionary or as I call it, Butchipedia:

> *Suspect:* One who is suspected; especially one who is suspected of a crime.
>
> *Contact:* A contact is someone who might have a need for the products or services you're selling. They are someone who you've introduced yourself to, who knows what you do, and how to reach you.
>
> *Prospect:* A prospect has demonstrated the desire for the products or services you are selling.

However, a prospect may or may not have the means with which to make that purchase.

In a perfect world contacts lead to prospects and prospects lead to clients.

Now that we have that out of the way, you should be making a minimum of *ten new* contacts each week. Who are these ten new contacts? Anybody.

You need to get out in the world. Meet people and have them meet you. Enjoy learning about others and truly develop an affection for this process and you'll scoff at making only ten new contacts a week.

How hard is this? Well, you probably made at least two or three today. But, did you realize they were contacts? The biggest issue here is recognizing the fact that from the time your feet hit the floor in the morning until you go to bed at night, you should at least be prepared to let someone know what you do and how to reach you. We meet people every day—in coffee shops, in line at the dry cleaners, on the train, or wherever. We strike up conversations with total strangers over the weather. I want you to start looking at these people as potential contacts. Be prepared to not only introduce yourself but to also give your own thirty-second commercial.

In his book, *The New Elevator Pitch*, author and speaker Chris Westfall (the National Elevator Pitch Champion) says your strongest opening "is the one that has the most direct appeal to your listener." As you probably already know everyone is running a mental software program that makes them ask, "What's in it for me?" and then, right after that, "Why should I care?"

He's so right. As you make these contacts and share your story, know your audience. The way you'd introduce yourself to an attorney is drastically different than how you'd get to know a farmer and his wife. They speak different languages and they process information differently. It's up to you to change—not them.

My introduction goes like this: "I'm Butch Bellah. I have my own training and development company where I am a speaker and sales trainer specializing in b2b sales. I work with individuals and organizations in that sector to help them get more appointments, win more business, and retain more customers."

That is a lot less than thirty seconds but it tells them everything I do. Then, I turn around and ask them what *they* do. It's important to let them know immediately that you are the expert we talked about in the opening of this book. You are the person who can solve problems. Now, I want to learn about them with a simple, "What kind of work do you do?" That one question will get people talking. If you have an opportunity, exchange business cards. (You should have a pocket full each day.)

One of the most useful habits is to track and log all these new contacts into a database. As you meet new people, keep up with them; who they are, what they do, where you met them, etc.

Start every Monday with a goal of making ten new contacts every week. That's a minimum of ten. If you make twelve one week—great, but you still have to make ten the following week. Granted, these are contacts and not necessarily prospects—but where do prospects come from? You should make it your personal mission, so that everyone you come in contact with knows who you are and what you do. You are your own walking advertisement. I don't care if you're an introvert or an extravert—you can make ten new contacts each week.

Make it a point to expand your sphere of influence and constantly be introducing yourself to new people. For example, if you stop at the same place for coffee every morning—find a new place. Find a place where you don't know anybody and then introduce yourself to everybody. Don't fall into the trap of visiting the same places every day for coffee, gas, lunch, etc. While we can become creatures of habit, those habits can inhibit your ability to grow your contact list. Choose your habits.

When you have a choice of two places to go—always choose the place where you know the fewest people. When all is said and done, we are talking about just two a day for a five-day work week. This is *not* difficult. I readily admitted in the beginning of this book that the strategies were going to be simple—but, you have to continue to do them week in and week out. You should have ten new contacts *every* week, not just this week.

You're probably saying, "This sounds like prospecting." It is. You're making contacts in hopes of uncovering prospects. Personally, I believe prospecting is overlooked by many sales coaches, authors, and trainers. I liken it to a sports coach teaching you the nuances of the game yet not telling you how to get to the stadium or field. I don't care how well you know how to play; if you have nobody to play with, it doesn't really matter, does it?

That's my goal here; to simply help you find ways to find someone to play with. So, take off the helmet or put down the bat. You're not going to need any of those things (as good as you may be at them) unless and until we get you someone to play with.

Now, notice I use the term "someone to play with" and not "an opponent." Having an opponent leads one to think there must be a winner and a loser and that is certainly not the case. Selling is something you do *for* someone not *to* someone. That change in mindset alone will make you more successful—and make more people want to play with you.

In many organizations the top salesperson is not the best closer—nor is it the person that works the longest hours or churns through the most potential customers. It's been my experience that

Building the Base

the truly successful salespeople—the true superstars are the ones who have mastered the skill of prospecting. Yet for some reason it is one of the last things new salespeople are trained to do—if at all. When, in fact, it should be the first thing they're trained to do.

Prospecting is both an art and a science, but also a learned skill—one that can be taught. And, with the help of the material I'm presenting here, one that I hope you will commit to learning and improving upon.

If one were to visualize the creation of the sales process it would begin with a suspect. Suspects *could* possibly be contacts, contacts *could* turn into prospects, and prospects will hopefully become customers. But, we have to start somewhere. And that somewhere is with suspects.

If you sell automobiles in Kalamazoo, then yes, the entire population of the earth is a suspect. But, we can eliminate those who either don't know how to or can't drive. Then, we can probably eliminate those who live outside the United States—unless you're a darned good car salesman and can get someone to travel overseas or across the border to buy your car. (If so, put this book down immediately and call me—we should be in business together somehow!)

Now, after that, you can probably eliminate suspects outside the state of Michigan or the surrounding states. Simple? Yes. But this is the process one goes through mentally and physically turning suspects into contacts into prospects.

I can't emphasize this enough; first start with everyone and then start eliminating those who don't fit the description.

When you're out and about, find areas of common interest to meet potential contacts. For example, sporting events, your children's activities, and neighborhood meetings are *great* places to meet *new* people. And that is truly what this is all about—meeting new people. Over simplified? Actually, no. In making these *ten* contacts a week it is all about simply meeting new people.

Another very powerful tool is to look at the people that you already do business with. Do they do business with you? Do they know what business you are in? Simply go through your checkbook or look at your debit card statement and see who you spend money with. Then, by all means, ensure they are aware of what you can do for them. They should immediately be added to your contact list.

You should also schedule at least one business mixer each month and get it on your calendar *now*. Whether its ribbon cuttings, chamber of commerce events, or other meetings you should go where there are people. Never miss an opportunity to let people know what business you are in—this also goes a long way to establishing yourself as the expert we talked about in the beginning. Be a joiner. Get involved in organizations that you can benefit from. But, be careful—I've found a few organizations who demand so much time it can become your job if you're not careful.

Volunteer. There are worthwhile charities and organizations in your own area that would love your help. Even if you never get a bit of business out of it, it's a great way to give back to your community. I highly encourage it.

Yet another strategy is to let your current customers help build your business. For example, find out who else sells to your customers. Meet and exchange information. How can you work together to grow both of your businesses? Simply leverage the relationships you already have. Furthermore, who are your customer's customers? How can you be of benefit to them and can they be contacts for you? The bottom line is almost anyone can be a contact—you just need to make *ten* new ones each week.

Finally, if you don't have a database—Microsoft Outlook or something—you are going to get left in the dust in today's business world. Keep up with these contacts; build your database and back it up constantly. This is where *tomorrow's* business will originate.

As you go through your day collect business cards, contact names, any touch point for a new contact. This is all information that you will log into your database. Record as much information on the new contact as you know; always keep up with how and where you met, if you were introduced by someone, or other information that reminds you of the encounter. Don't leave these details to chance or try to remember them. As this contact list grows, there is no way you can possibly remember all that you will need to know about these people.

There are numerous apps for scanners or for smart phones that record all the information off a business card just by taking a picture of it. There's no excuse not to collect this information.

Let's not forget these people are contacts. They are not prospects—yet. Perhaps some of them will be. Hopefully, many of them will be. But the beauty of this system is that you will find the more contacts you make, the more prospects you have.

Simple stuff, huh? But, are you walking the walk or just talking the talk?

One final point: *Do not* just collect names or meet people that you think you can eventually sell to. Meet *everyone*! While they may not be a potential customer, their brother-in-law could be or their next door neighbor may be in need of your products or services. Plus, these are people that you will one day be able to help in one form or another—it may not be a sale, but it will be something. If you go into it with that in mind, you will breeze through adding ten contacts to your database *every* week.

Newsflash: *Ten* new contacts per week equals five hundred new contacts each year!

಄

**Each contact with a human being is so rare,
so precious, one should preserve it.
~Anais Nin**

Developing Tomorrow's Sales

Habit #2
Create a Top Ten List and Review It Daily

After developing this habit, you will be able to easily track your ten hottest prospects and keep moving them toward a sale. Honestly, this one should be a "gimme." You already have—or should have—ten good, *hot* prospects in your sales pipeline. If not, don't worry about it. We are going to give you the tools it takes to build this key piece of your arsenal.

What is a Top Ten list? It is simply a list of the ten prospects most likely to buy from you in the shortest time frame. You should list the prospects in order of your belief in their ability to become a customer; meaning the number one position on your Top Ten list should be held by your *best* prospect. The second position by the second best and so on. You should constantly be updating this list.

No matter what your product or service is, there are steps to a sale. From the initial contact through asking for the sale, follow up, and ultimately retaining the customer—there are steps along the way. Completing a sale is a journey and the Top Ten list simply allows you to see at a glance how far along each of your hottest prospects are.

The key to successfully employing your Top Ten list is to review it daily. You should be brutally honest with yourself about where the relationships with these prospects stand. Are they moving forward? If not, why? What needs to be done with any single one of them to move them forward toward a sale or closer to building the relationship that will ultimately result in a sale? What can you do today to progress on to the next step in the process?

Now, here's a word of caution. This is not a wish list; this is not a list of potential customers you'd like to have or you hope to meet one day. These are genuine hot prospects who can and should be closed in very short order—and remember, they should be ranked based on their ability to be closed. This makes it very easy for you during your review alone or with a manager to make decisions on where your time and energy should be spent.

We all have prospects who we can't seem to "pull across the hump." We get them right up to the end of the process and they stall, for whatever reason. If that's the case, get a manager involved and discuss the situation and decide what needs to be done in order to convert that prospect to a customer.

Once you have this list and are honestly working it, this list should be reviewed weekly with your sales manager. When you have any meeting with your manager, bring your Top Ten list. How can he or she help you close prospect No. 1? How can your manager assist you in moving prospect No. 7 farther on their journey to becoming a customer and into position No. 6? All of that information is readily available if you are maintaining this list and reviewing it daily. A note to sales managers: This should be required of every salesperson at every sales meeting.

Again, since there are steps to a sale, each of these prospects on your Top Ten list will be at a different stage. That's okay. The key here is to focus on moving each relationship forward—constantly.

Now, if you don't have ten good, hot prospects (be honest), make it a point over the next few weeks to fill up your list. As you make presentations and present your product or services, honestly assess where (and if) the prospect should be on your Top Ten list. There are many people you call on who will not be on this list. Just because you made a presentation and they are "in the hopper" certainly doesn't automatically qualify them for this list. Are they one of your ten hottest prospects? It's a simple yes or no. If so, where do they belong on the list?

This is a fluid, living document and it is yours and yours alone. Nobody can tell you who should or should not be on the list and where they should rank. Just because Prospect A is in position No. 1 this week, doesn't mean they should automatically be there next week. If something happens with the prospect in position No. 2 to make them the hottest prospect, then they should be No. 1. In a perfect world, your next sale should always be the person at the top of your Top Ten list.

If these potential clients that occupy your Top Ten list are truly your best prospects, don't they deserve to be treated that way? You bet! Everyone—yes, everyone—on your Top Ten list should hear from you every week in one form or another. If the prospect is truly deserving of being on the list, they are deserving of contact, conversation, and work. Don't you agree?

This is where it becomes painfully obvious if you're spending time and energy with a prospect or even a contact who is draining your resources and which should be spent on people who will eventually be your customer. Once you begin to use this beautifully simply tool to its maximum effectiveness, your Top Ten list will become the most important piece of data you have. If the building were on fire and all you could save was one thing—grab your Top Ten List! It truly is that important. You should treat it like tomorrow's pay check, because that's exactly what it is.

The beauty of this Power of Ten system is that eventually you will have a secondary list just waiting for a spot to open up on that all important Top Ten list. It's like the old Ferris wheel example—when one seat empties, load it up again and keep it moving. As one of these Top Ten becomes a customer, there should be a waiting list to get on.

Keep your list with you at all times—even when you are in the field. If you have five minutes between appointments, get your Top Ten list out and think about what you can do today to move the relationships forward. What can you do today to create new business from this list? What can you do today to help one of these potential clients solve their problems and fill their needs?

The single biggest benefit is that this tool allows you to eliminate what I consider to be the biggest hurdle keeping professional salespeople from being successful—spending time and energy on prospects who will never buy. Professional salespeople ascend to the top of their profession by maximizing the use of their sales time. If you study the top producers in any industry you'll find they do very little—if anything—during their sales hours that doesn't help them convert prospects to customers.

By far the biggest time-waster for most salespeople is one we bring on ourselves. It's not something others dump on us or tasks that we find to keep ourselves busy. The biggest time-waster we have (and the one that needs to be eliminated most) is hanging onto prospects that will never buy no matter what we do. We're trained to continue to close, follow up, close, follow up, close, and follow up. We call and call and call—leaving voice mail after voice mail—knowing deep down inside that the work we're doing will never result in a sale.

As salespeople—we're focused on selling and not turning prospects loose. But, how many sales could you make if you spent this wasted time working with potential customers that could and should eventually buy?

One of the strategies I teach, and believe in whole-heartedly, is that there are times when we—as professionals—must fire prospects. Yes, you read correctly—fire them. There comes a time when it's no longer prudent to continue to call on someone that isn't going to buy. That time could be spent with a new prospect or with a current customer that deserves your attention. So, how do you do this—and when is the time?

When calling for a prospect, I will leave four very specific voice mails before I leave my final voice mail. And, when I say final—I mean final. After the fifth voice mail, I will not call the prospect back. What I say on this final voice mail is almost verbatim:

> *Mr./Mrs. Prospect, this is Butch Bellah again at (my cell phone number). I've left a couple of voice mails and have been unable to reach you. I know you're busy and so am I, so I won't bother you again. I'm not going to continue to bug you. If you'd like to reach me, my number is (insert your number here). Again, I'm not going to bother you anymore. Thanks.*

First, I acknowledge that the prospect is busy, but so am I. Second, I use the words "bug" and "bother" intentionally. I'm not really sure why, but they seem to have always worked for me. What have I accomplished? I've let the prospect know that we are about to end the voice mail circle and put the ball in their court. Are they really a prospect? Believe it or not, more than 50% of the prospects that receive this message will call me back with, "Butch, I had lost your number," or, "I've been meaning to call you back, but I got swamped."

Whatever their issue is, I don't care. They will call you back and now is your chance to try to get on their calendar and start the relationship.

What is key is that I eliminate this prospect from my prospect list after this final voice mail. After you leave this voice mail, do not call back! You are a professional and your time is valuable, too.

David Letterman has made a lot of money with a Top Ten list and you can, too.

Finally, keep in mind these are prospects you are actively working. These are people you have at least established some rapport with and are working to make them a future customer. If you don't have ten in your pipeline today, don't worry about it. Get out there, make your contacts, make your presentations and develop the rest of your list.

But, if you don't have ten a month from today. Who's to blame for that?

☙
**You have to do what others won't.
To achieve what others don't.
~Anonymous**

Gaining an Extra Week Each Year

Habit #3
Get To Work Ten Minutes Early

It doesn't get much more basic than this; get to work earlier. Many studies have shown the most successful people in this world make the most of their morning time. So, in order to get this freight train of positive momentum moving in your direction, you need to be at work ten minutes earlier every day. I'm not asking you to work around the clock or stay up till the wee hours of the morning. Ten minutes—that's all I ask.

Have you ever heard "You must be present to win"? Well, it's not just for bingo and raffles anymore. Think about that sentence. If your business opens at 8:00 a.m. get there at 7:50 a.m. If you normally come in at 7:30 a.m., try 7:20 a.m.

If a potential customer was standing outside your office with checkbook in hand—waiting for you to unlock the door tomorrow morning—how long would it take you to be ready? If you have to do anything except flip on the light switch, you need to be better prepared. And preparation is what those additional ten minutes are all about! In those ten minutes you are going to prepare to succeed, prepare for a positive day in which you will make an impact.

Think about this for a moment; an extra ten minutes every day adds up to more than one full work-week per year! Now, what could you accomplish if you had an extra week when your competition was closed? Seriously, consider that. You have the entire market to yourself. No competition anywhere in sight—just you. Do you think you could grow your business? Do you think you could increase your sales and create separation between you and the rest of the field?

I would think so!

Here's the best part; your competition is probably not even aware you're open while they are closed! And if they're like most people these days, they're dragging in late instead of on time.

Ten minutes. Ten minutes that will set the tone for how you attack your day and become the expert in your field. But, if you use those ten minutes to read the newspaper or play on the internet or find other ways to waste time, just stay home. There's no sense in running up the company's electricity bill if you're not making the best use of the time.

Use the extra time to prepare yourself mentally and physically for your sales day. Make it a point to see how much you can accomplish in those ten minutes. If your business is like most, there probably won't be a quieter, more peaceful time of day. The phone won't be ringing and others won't be stopping by your desk to chit-chat.

This is a perfect time to enter data from the previous day's calls and contacts, formulate strategies for presentations, and any number of non-selling tasks. This is the time to make copies, fill out call reports, and other required paperwork. We want to spend our sales time out doing things which directly lead to sales, so this is the time to get the other minutia out of the way. Repeat—do not waste time when you could either be in front of a prospect, making a presentation, prospecting, or selling by doing menial tasks that could and should be performed during your down time.

You should always review your schedule for the day. Do you have all the essential materials ready? If you are traveling to a sales call, do you know where you are going? (Don't laugh—we've all been guilty of this one.)

For years I've talked to sales teams and groups about this one single, simple technique; get to work ten minutes early. In the beginning, (almost) everyone finds it humorous. Some question whether I'm serious. Let me assure you, I could not be more serious. In my personal career I've found this to be one of—if not the most powerful—techniques I've ever employed.

Ten minutes early. Can you do it? Absolutely. But, you have to do it consistently! Start creating this habit now!

The goal is to separate yourself from your competition—give yourself any possible edge. If you're coming in ten minutes early, don't make up for it by leaving ten minutes early. Finish your day and finish it strong.

A pet peeve of mine is the behavior around Monday and Friday sales. Most of your competition drags in late on Monday and leaves early on Friday—essentially working at best a four day work week. Don't join that crowd. I can assure you that your weekend will be much more rewarding and relaxing if you are celebrating a sale and not just dreading Monday rolling around.

Let's face it, Monday is 20% of your sales week—I personally, don't have the luxury of wasting one fifth of my time. I would much prefer to be out there meeting with customers and prospects while my competition is lulled to sleep.

Fridays are just as bad, if not worse. Ah, Friday. Everyone's favorite day of the week; the end of the work week and the start of the weekend. Well, for most people. We all know about TGIF and "Hang on Baby, Friday's Comin'!" but you really should look forward to this day for other reasons, as well.

A friend of mine used to say every week, "It's Friday, baby!" and you could tell by the way he said it there was no doubt about him being ready for the weekend.

But, I've found Friday to be a great day to close sales. In fact, I've found it to be one of the best. Why? Well, for one thing the majority of your competition has already switched onto auto-pilot and they are literally coasting through the day. I've met some people that actually hoped they didn't get a call about a potential sale on Friday. What? Are you kidding me?

Conversely there are some buyers that tend to take the day off, as well. I understand that. But, that just means the ones that are working are ready to do business. They're professional and value their time and yours, too.

If you are a sports fan, you know that in football quarterbacks are judged many times on what they do in the fourth quarter. At the same time, baseball pays a lot of money to closers (interesting term, huh?)—pitchers who are brought in simply to pitch the final inning and close the game.

You are the quarterback and the closer; Friday is your fourth quarter and ninth inning and the game is yours to win.

Look at it this way; most (not all) of your competitors have given you one fifth of the week where the market is wide open—

it's all yours! They've got their feet up watching the clock and counting the hours until they can start their weekend. And I want to thank every single one of them!

So, the next time somebody says, "It's Friday, baby!" You can smile all the way to the top of your profession!

Also, the next time you are trying to close a sale on a Friday, try this close. Say, "Let's go ahead and get this wrapped up before the weekend." Simple? Yes. Effective? You better believe it!

But, back to the ten extra minutes. The bottom line is that these ten minutes should be used to ensure you are ready to make the day as successful as possible. These valuable ten minutes can and will add up providing you with an unseen advantage over your competition. Use it wisely. Remember, your time is the most valuable asset you have. Don't waste it!

If you'll commit to start doing this tomorrow, you will soon be looking forward to this extra time because of how productive you are. (And you won't be standing over the printer or copy machine in a cold sweat at the last minute preparing for a presentation.)

ಬ

Hard work spotlights the character of people: some turn up their sleeves, some turn up their noses and some don't turn up at all.
-Sam Ewing

Goals—Setting and Focusing on Them

Habit #4
Read Your Goals Aloud Ten Times Every Day

Goals. Sadly, to some salespeople they're a myth, a fable, an old-wives' tale. I can't count the number of salespeople over the years when I asked to see their goals for the month, the quarter, or the year who have told me, "I know them, but I don't have them written down or anything." Granted, there is a lot of misinformation out there on goals—the Harvard (or Yale) Research Study of 1953 or 1979 never happened.

But, here's my question: If there is even a hint that committing your goals to writing gives you the slightest advantage, why not take it? It's not like its hard work or anything. You're simply writing your goals on a piece of paper—a piece of paper than can only be seen by you. Nobody said you had to tattoo them on your forehead—they are for your benefit.

Do you have a To Do list for today? If so, why? If you're like me it's because you simply want to make sure you can quickly glance at things you want to get done today or in short order. If I don't write it down, I might forget it. Then let me ask you, if it's important enough to write down who you need to call today or to pick up milk on the way home from work, don't you think it's important enough to write down what you want to make sure you accomplish this month, this quarter or even over the next one, three, or five-year period?

This fourth habit is all about reading your goals ten times every day. But, admittedly before one can read them they must be written down. If you haven't written them down, let's do that now. (Go ahead, I'll wait.)

You don't have to have twenty or even ten, you can start with just three things; one thing you want to accomplish this month, one thing you want to accomplish this quarter, and one thing you want to accomplish this year.

Use the S.M.A.R.T. test on all your goals. There are several variations, but this is the one I prefer:

- Specific
- Measurable
- Attainable
- Relevant
- Time Bound

Make sure they meet those criteria. Also, when writing your goals, write them as "I will" instead of "I want." For example, if your goal is to sell fifty units this month your goal should read, "I will sell fifty (whatever you sell) before the end of (month). That is much more powerful than, "I want to sell fifty . . . ." When reading that each day you are instilling in your brain the fact that you will achieve that goal.

Now that we've gotten them written down, let's talk about our original task—reading them ten times every day.

Goals—Setting and Focusing on Them

Here are a few tips for you if you think you'll struggle with finding ten opportunities a day to do this.

We've probably all heard about taping them to the bathroom mirror so you see them every morning. While some may find that silly or juvenile or whatever, I would be willing to bet in many cases where that strategy has been employed, the bathroom was bigger than my first home!

Another handy way to see these goals is to make a copy of your list and tape it to the sun visor in your car. Whenever you get in—make it a habit—before you ever put the car into gear, flip the visor down and read them. If you are like a lot people, that's going to get you a minimum of four times a day. To and from work and to and from lunch. But, if you work out of your car, you can get all ten in just by flipping that visor down. It's very powerful and in the time when your brain is most accepting of the information. Consider this, if you come out of a sales call and have just been beaten to a pulp by the prospect—and we all know it happens—isn't that a great time to remind yourself what you are in this for?

Conversely, if you are leaving a sales call where you've just signed up a trophy account or perhaps landed the biggest account of your career—then take a look at those goals. The next prospect you call on is already sold.

Still another way to see and read these daily is to make your list of goals your screen saver on your computer. You'll see that several times a day.

It's all about creating good habits. We all have plenty of bad habits we've developed over our lifetime, put a little effort into creating some good ones. Written goals are essential to your success and reading them ten times a day will cement them into your psyche and allow your subconscious mind to work for you. Ralph Waldo Emerson said, "Once you make a decision, the universe conspires to make it happen." By reading your goals daily—you're mentally making that decision.

In fact a study by Dr. Gail Matthews found that people who commit their goals to writing and share weekly updates with a friend or accountability partner are 33% more likely to achieve those goals. The study quoted Dr. Matthews as saying, "My study provides empirical evidence for the effectiveness of three coaching tools: accountability, commitment, and writing down one's goals."

I don't know about you, but anything that gives me a third better chance of success for such a small physical effort is hard to ignore! By practicing this habit you'll hold yourself accountable.

When the first quarter ends are you 25% of the way toward your annual goal? If not, what must happen for you to get back on track? If you read it at the beginning of June you know you only have one month to hit the midway point of the year; these little mile-markers serve as a reminder as to not only where you're going, but how close you are to getting there. If you've ever run a race or participated in a similar event you know the value of being able to imagine the finish line. Visualize achievement. Visualize success. Visualize winning.

Finally, note that this habit says to read your goals aloud. Yes, that means out loud. You can do it in the privacy of your own home, car, office, or wherever but the key here is use your auditory senses as much as your visual ones. Not only are you seeing yourself achieve your goals ten times a day, you're hearing it as well. And, who knows; if you see it and hear it enough you might just start to believe it!

Goals—Setting and Focusing on Them

ಬ
If you want to live a happy life, tie it to a goal, not to people or things.
~Albert Einstein

Getting Past the Gatekeeper and Getting on Their Calendar

Habit #5
Develop Ten New Prospects of Your Own Each Month

In this chapter, we're going to address the heart and soul of your sales success; your ability to get to see potential clients. We will delve deeply into the art of setting appointments (although we'll learn to stop using that terminology) and getting past the gatekeeper when you're being blocked from talking to a prospect.

It's no secret that many salespeople who work by appointment calling on prospective customers struggle to get an audience—and just setting the initial appointment can be one of the hardest parts of the sales process. Today I want to address some things I've learned over the years that have made a huge difference for me and they will for you to—if you use them.

Understand that you and I could make a phone call to the exact same prospect five minutes apart selling the exact same product or service and one of us could get an appointment while the other strikes out, right? I believe it all boils down to one simple thing—the words we use. By changing the words we use we can drastically increase the percentage of appointments set in a call cycle. Do you agree? I'm not talking about being deceptive; I'm talking about choosing good, positive words instead of ones that have proven to be less successful in setting the appointment.

For starters remove the word "appointment" from your vocabulary. Get rid of it *today*! Just the word has negative connotations.

- Attorneys require appointments.
- You make a doctor's appointment when you're sick.
- You make an appointment with your dentist when you have a toothache.
- You make an appointment with a proctologist . . . well, never mind (see it's very negative)

So, if you're not going to use the "A" word what do we do? Replace it with this, "I'd like to get on your calendar." That's it.

No longer are you going to ask a prospect for an appointment, rather you are going to try to "get on their calendar." I learned this simple technique several years ago and the results are amazing. (I hope I am giving proper credit when I tell you I learned it from a book by the great Stephan Schiffman—at least I think that's where it came from.)

Next we are going to replace the phrase or verbiage about "presentations" with the word "visit," as in "I'd like to get on your calendar one day next week and stop by to visit with you." That one sentence alone will get you in front of more prospects than you would ever believe. But, you must use it. And, I highly suggest using it verbatim. (But, planned not canned.) If we're asking to visit instead of making a presentation, walls come down—doors open up. It's just that simple. People hate presentations, but they love to visit. They visit with friends, family, and neighbors. More than likely they sit around the kitchen table over coffee and visit.

It is a much more intimate form of communication. And just the word alone inspires feelings drastically different from the dreaded "presentation." Again, this changes *nothing* about what I'm going to do when I get to see the prospect it just greatly enhances my chance to *get* to see them.

So, the conversation would go something like this, (I like to be very low-key and not sound like every other salesperson that calls on someone) "Hey, Mr. Smith (or Bob, if the situation allows it) this is Butch Bellah calling and I wanted to see if I could get on your calendar for one day next week and stop in and visit with you for a few minutes?"

One of the main things to note is that when I deliver this sentence, I don't sound like I am asking a question. My voice inflection is such that I *expect* to "get on his calendar." I don't frame it as a question—it's much more light and conversational. Just as if you'd ask a friend, "Hey, how about we visit over coffee Monday?" Technically, that's a question. But, the way it comes out of your mouth is more of an assumed statement.

Write this down: "Hey, Mr. Smith this is _____ calling and I want to see if I can get on your calendar for one day next week and stop in and visit with you for a few minutes?"

Rehearse. Rehearse. Rehearse it. And then, rehearse it some more. Record it and then play it back to make sure you are delivering it in a way that is audible, and in a way that you expect for your request to be fulfilled. Make it clear and *make it sound natural* and you will be amazed by the results.

Simply, by using "get on their calendar" you will be able to hear the prospect flipping pages in their calendar or clicking on their computer to see what they have scheduled. It is truly a very powerful statement.

In some cases the prospect will ask what I want to visit about. And that's fine. If I'm asked that question, I respond with the following—verbatim, "Well, I've got some ideas and I want to pick your brain for a little bit." Wait. What? I want to pick his brain? Absolutely.

Many times you'll get a chuckle with, "there's not much to pick," or something along those lines, but you are breaking down walls with every sentence. Do not lose sight of the fact that these need to be delivered casually in a conversational, not selling, manner.

If pressed farther, I'll even tell the prospect, "Well, I've been doing a little research and I wanted to get your thoughts on some ways we might work together."

Again, I've not lied or been deceptive, and when someone asks if I'm trying to sell something, I will readily admit that I am. *Never* lie or dodge the question. But, if you use the strategy above you will soon have *your* calendar full!

Unless you run into…*the gatekeeper* (cue the scary music).

Ah, the beloved gatekeeper; the person standing between you and your potential prospect. I propose we start by changing that thought. The gatekeeper is not there to keep you from the prospect, he or she is there to keep your competition from the prospect—and once they become your client you will love this person.

Start today to change the way you see their role. It is not to keep you out, it's to keep others out.

With that being said, we all have to deal with these people and I've found a few methods that work extremely well. In fact, I would suggest you use some of these strategies word for word.

Memorize them, but make them sound natural—use voice inflection and tonality to make your conversation sound as if you're simply having a conversation.

I realize that often you're faced with the challenge of even getting to talk to the person you're trying to sell. In fact the process usually goes something like this:

1. Reach the gatekeeper
2. Find a way past, around, or through the gatekeeper
3. Leave a message for the decision maker
4. Leave another message for the decision maker
5. Ask the gatekeeper's advice for reaching the decision maker

You know the drill.

Again, I love gatekeepers. I absolutely adore them and I'm dead serious. Remember, they keep competitors away from my customers and keep other salespeople (who give up too easily or don't have the proper skills) from reaching the decision makers that I'm trying to sell.

Not so bad, are they? If you have the right skills and know how to handle them, they actually perform a very useful service.

So, let's go through some strategies and tips on how to make them your friend and ally, which will allow you to reach more decision makers!

First, I'm going to assume you know who the buyer is at the company you are calling on. If not, the gatekeeper is *not* the person to ask. The red flag goes *way* up when you have to call them to find out. You should use the internet, networking, or any number of other methods to learn the *name* of the person you are trying to reach prior to calling. Furthermore, do not call and ask for "who handles the buying." Big no-no.

Okay, for the sake of discussion, let's say that we are going to try to reach Bob Smith by calling; we want to get on his calendar so we can stop by and visit. Here's how we handle it.

When the gatekeeper picks up, your voice inflection should suggest that you are calling an old friend or family member. Be relaxed and low key!

"Who's speaking?" you ask.

If they say, "Who are you trying to reach?" I simply say this, "It's Butch. I was calling for Bob." Notice that I didn't say Bob Smith or Mr. Smith, etc. I'm treating this like I'm calling an old friend who I've called a hundred times.

However, nine times out of ten the gatekeeper will answer your initial question with, "This is Sherry," to which you reply (again, very naturally), "Oh, hey Sherry, its Butch, is Bob around?" Now, several things happen here:

1. Sherry thinks she is supposed to recognize my voice (trust me)

2. I didn't ask to speak to Bob or if Mr. Smith was in or anything very formal—I simply asked if Bob was around

3. Sherry assumes Bob and I know each other and that we've spoken before (again, trust me)

4. Sherry will almost feel as if Bob will be mad at her if she doesn't put through the call from

his friend, Butch (trust me—I've done it hundreds of times).

This is not rocket science and I am *not* being deceitful. If Sherry asks, "Is Bob expecting your call?" I will almost chuckle and answer with this, "Well, probably not today, I was just going to pick his brain for a second."

Again, I've not lied about anything. I've just put her at ease that I am someone she should put through to Bob. Remember to keep expectation in the tone of your voice.

If Bob is not in and/or Sherry wants to take a message, I end with this, "Just tell him Butch called I'll give him a buzz later." Again, this is natural and friendly. Now, *write down* Sherry's name because the next time you call, you are going to say, "Hey Sherry, its Butch did I catch Bob in this afternoon?" Now you know *both* of them.

And with this, she really feels as if you're someone she should put through.

If you will learn this strategy and use it effortlessly and naturally, your success rate of getting past gatekeepers will increase dramatically. In fact, I'm going to say you that will be *shocked* at how easy it is to reach the decision maker—and you will come to love those gatekeepers that keep the others out!

ಐ

The brick walls are there to give us a chance to show how badly we want something. Because the brick walls are there to stop the people who don't want it badly enough.
~Dr. Randy Pausch

Keeping Your Current Clients Happy

Habit #6
Contact Ten Current or Past Customers Monthly

As one make's their way through their sales day, week, and month it is easy to get caught up in hitting new business numbers, call reports numbers, and so forth. While all of those are important, the easiest sale you'll ever make is to someone who is already buying from you. But, in order to do that you must maintain an ongoing relationship with that customer after they become a customer.

I train and coach salespeople to consciously make contact (in person if at all possible) with current and/or past customers every month. My magic number once again is ten per month. Never get so caught up in chasing a potential sale that you find yourself losing a current customer because you failed to follow up, handle a problem, or took them for granted.

Let's first talk about the bad stuff. Yes, bad things happen to good salespeople. All the time.

Let's face it; errors are part of business. Orders are mishandled, products are damaged or shipped incorrectly, and deliveries are late. The larger the business you represent the more it happens and the more one has to learn to satisfy dissatisfied customers. While I believe you should always strive for perfection, the reality is we are all going to have customers who are upset for one reason or another. How you handle those customers will go a long way in determining how successful you will be.

Everyone can keep happy customers. But, what you do with the unhappy ones is the difference between a good salesperson and a superstar.

Years ago I learned one simple phrase that will solve many customer's problems, yet is much too seldom used. When a customer has a problem, simply use the following statement, "I'm sorry we've put you or your company in that position, what would you like me to do to solve the problem?"

Basically, seven words that can turn any situation around, "What would you like me to do?"

Here is the amazing thing about using that phrase; in most cases what the customer asks you to do is *less* than what you would've done in the first place. Many times, they just want you to show concern and be aware of the problem.

"What would you like me to do?" Use it and the results will surprise you.

The other thing to keep in mind is that errors in business are opportunities to show customer's how much you care and how you respond to such challenges. This is not the time to place blame, it's time to solve the problem and make it right for the customer.

One of the main ingredients in high customer satisfaction is how we manage their expectations. If we do that correctly, many times we can minimize or totally eliminate their dissatisfaction with a particular situation. While we may not be able to eliminate the problems that occur, we can control how we handle them with the customer.

Keeping Your Clients Happy

The key is communication.

If your customer thinks delivery of their product will be Tuesday and you know it won't be until Thursday, by all means tell them ahead of time. Bad news does not get easier with time—it gets harder. We've all heard, "under promise and over deliver." Again, that requires communication for you to under promise in the first place. It is far better to be ahead of a deadline than behind.

If you know a price increase is coming, notify your customer as soon as possible. The worst thing that can happen is to have that information come from the market—or worse, a competitor.

Communicate. Communicate. Communicate.

I've seen many salespeople at the point of a sale (or shortly thereafter) have a customer ask for something that is impossible. But, afraid they're going to lose the sale—they promise it or agree to it anyway—thinking they can deal with it later. Wrong. Manage the customer's expectations at every turn—including and especially at the time of the initial sale.

If you know your production department is going to take forty-eight hours to complete an order, tell the customer seventy-two hours. Remember, it's better to be early and give yourself some buffer rather than sweating that last half day waiting . . . hoping . . . praying it's going to work out.

Never lose a sale to a competitor because of mismanaged customer expectations. It is one thing you have complete control over. We all have times where for whatever reason we fall short of a customer's expectations and of our standards. We mess up. Things happen. Nobody's perfect.

But, how you handle that situation is the difference between a true professional and one who aspires to be one. Over the years, one of the keys that I've found is to simply tell the customer what you *can* do instead of what you *can't* do.

It's just that simple.

If you've missed a delivery date, instead of telling them what you aren't capable of—just tell them what you can do to make it right. Don't focus on the negative, lean toward the positive. Have an order for a customer get fouled up? Instead of telling them all the ways you can't solve their problem, how about focusing on the ways you can?

The customer's attitude and acceptance is drastically different based on how you approach the situation. As salespeople, we all have fires to put out from time to time—but, are you fanning the flames or putting the fire out? Your reaction, attitude, and willingness to solve the problem dictates in large part how the customer views the issue.

Make it better. Not worse.

With that being said, no matter how easy the fix is for you—it could be as simple as repacking an order—don't convey to the customer that it was no big deal. Without boasting or throwing it up in the customer's face, you should not be afraid to take credit for solving the problem. Sadly today, it doesn't take much to stand out. You want the customer to know they can depend on you—but they should also feel like that because they know you will do *anything* to solve their problem, not that it was not a problem in the first place.

As you grow your business and strive to get better—learn to embrace mistakes, learn from them, and use them as opportunities to separate yourself from your competition. Keep your cool and don't get stressed over things where you have no control. You will do a much better job of solving problems when you approach them with that attitude.

I am not advocating you wait until something goes wrong or potentially could go wrong to reach out to a current customer. In fact, I hope you more frequently talk to them when there aren't any issues to deal with.

We've all heard the sayings, "knowledge is power" and "the one with the most data wins." Well, not only is that true, but in today's world it's critical to your success. In order to achieve that ultra-level of success and truly be a difference maker, one must know their customer better than anyone—and in some cases know them better than they know themselves.

While we can go on and on and on about asking questions and interviewing prospects and customers, there are ways to learn more about them without grilling them. For instance, what can you learn about your customer's business? Are there trade magazines that your clients read? If so, the next time you call on one and see a copy of *Underwater Basket Weaving Monthly*, ask if you can have a copy. There is always a subscription card for you to get your own copies in the future. Know what your customers know—read what they read. Understand their industry and what challenges they face and you will automatically begin to be able to fill needs easier and better than your competition.

What about trade shows? What trade shows do your customers' attend? Is it worth going as an exhibitor or just as a guest? Perhaps. If you're selling medical supplies, find out what trade shows or conventions are held for the industry and be there. You can learn a lot and meet a lot of potential clients there. (I know this one sounds basic, but you would not believe the number of salespeople that *completely* miss this opportunity.)

Are there associations you can join as an associate member or supporting member? If there is a National Association of Underwater Basket Weavers, you should find out about associate membership and how it can help you stay connected with what's important to your customer.

Finally, what online blogs, websites, and newsletters come to your customer? Do an online search for the industry and see what's out there. You'll be surprised at some of the specialized content available—and much of it is free.

One of the nice things about reading trade magazines is when you notice one of your customers being recognized or featured. You should always look for those opportunities to separate yourself from the pack. A nice framed copy of the article with a small note congratulating them on their achievement can go a long way!

Be on the lookout for articles, business changes, and other pertinent news which affect your customers. In that instance, pick up the phone and call. "Bob, it's Butch, I just noticed one of your competitors is closing up shop and wanted to see if there is anything I can do to help you gain some of their accounts?" Or how about this, "Hey Janet, it's Butch. I was surfing the net and noticed something about a fire at a plant in Argentina. Is that going to affect your business and if so, what can I do to help?"

Your call should always be centered around, "How can I help?" Find ways to help your customers grow their business and they will help you grow yours!

Finally, if you're not contacting lost or orphaned customers, you're cheating yourself. If you lose a customer (and everyone does), do you know why? Don't you want to know? If so, ask. "Where did I foul up?" "What did we do to upset you?" "What was it that caused you to change suppliers?" "Why did you chose that to switch to X?"

Find out. These answers will not only open the door for conversations with those customers but they could certainly help you prevent the same mistakes from occurring in the future.

One of the biggest issues with lost customers is they never want to look like they've made a bad decision to leave you—even if they have. Make it your job to allow them to come back and become a customer again without having to grovel or save face.

This is huge.

I will almost guarantee you there are customers today who you've lost who would come back if you made it easy for them to do so. But, they don't want to look like they are having to come crawling back to you. Even if you were 100% right and they were 100% wrong, you have 0% of their business as long as you make switching back an issue. Get over it. It's not worth it.

If I lost a customer—for whatever reason—one of the last things I would leave them with is something to the effect of, "John, I hate that I let you down. I realize it wasn't an easy decision for you and I'm sorry I put you in that position. But, if you find out the grass isn't necessarily greener on the other side, all you have to do is call me and I'll be 'Johnny-On-The-Spot' ready to pick up where we left off and I assure you I'll do a better job in the future."

Now, what have I done?

First, I've taken the blame for whatever made the customer leave (even if it wasn't personally my fault), I've acknowledged I put them in a tough position (even if it wasn't, I now have the customer thinking that way) and finally I've made it perfectly clear that in the event they get to the other side and it's not all roses, I will gladly welcome them back.

I've allowed the customer to save face. Never make it hard to do business with you—especially for someone who has already done business with you.

If you make a habit of contacting ten current and/or lost customers each month you'll be pleased with what you find. Opportunities are everywhere and some of them are right in front of your eyes. Current customers may have issues or even referrals (we'll talk about that when we discuss Habit #9) and orphaned customers may just be looking for any reason at all to come back. Give them a reason.

~

Spend a lot of time talking to customers face to face. You'd be amazed how many companies don't listen to their customers.
~Ross Perot

Preparing To Succeed

Habit #7
Learn Closes for Your Ten Most Common Objections

While I don't personally believe there is any one single step in the sales process that is more important than another, there are two places where many salespeople struggle—asking for the sale and then overcoming objections. I would be doing you—the reader—a disservice if we didn't cover the art of asking for the sale.

And yes, it is an art. And, this is the perfect place to delve into it before we cover how to overcome those objections.

Everybody wants to be a better closer—but unless you do everything else right before that, your sales will not improve.

Closing is a learned process. As the late Zig Ziglar once said, "I've never opened the paper and read where a woman gave birth to an 8 lb. 9 oz. salesman." You need to be great—not just good—great at building rapport before you move on to the next step. Then you need to be very proficient and comfortable with introducing and getting commitment with a verbal contract prior to going any further.

Personally, I promote an eight-step sales process. It is very much like climbing a ladder; if you miss a rung, the next step could be really painful.

There are so many different beliefs, strategies, and ideas on how to ask for the sale (I really prefer not to call it closing) that I could probably write a new book every day for a month and tackle it from a different direction. And, at the end of that month you and I both would be so confused we wouldn't be able to spell "sale," much less ask for one.

In a bit, I'm going to give you a technique I personally use and learned from Hugh Liddle of Red Cap Sales Coaching. This is one I can endorse, and tell you without question that it works. Then we'll discuss a technique for having great closes at your disposal when needed. However, before we get into that, there are a couple of other aspects I consider just as important as the words you use.

First and foremost is confidence. One builds confidence through repetition, practice, and a general knowledge of what you are going to say. For example, if you have a scripted, well-rehearsed, natural-sounding way of asking for the sale, your confidence will be exponentially higher than if you are winging it. (Never wing it.)

Second, it is important that when you come to the part of the sales process where you do ask for the sale, don't change anything. Don't change your body language, how you're positioned, or your approach to the customer. If anything, the level of your voice should drop slightly, your speech pattern slowed, and the inflection and passion in your voice should be increased. But this should be authentic; it is all about sincerity.

So, what should you say? Obviously this depends greatly on your product or service, so I'm going to have to give you a general script out of necessity. You can easily adapt this to your specific business. I want you to read this and then read it again and again and again. Memorize it. But, memorize it in a way where you can

Preparing to Succeed

deliver it as naturally as you do your name. Again, you shouldn't give any signal to your prospect that something is about to change (i.e. I'm about to ask you to buy!)

> Mr. Prospect, you've said you like our product and it will solve the problem you're having with tracking the turnaround time of your monthly reports. Here's the best part—I've got two options for you! Option one would include installation, a twelve-month maintenance package and full technical support for just $12,500 (pronounced "twelve-five").
>
> Option two also includes installation, but comes with a thirty-six-month maintenance package and full technical support for just $15,500 (pronounced 'fifteen-five") saving you almost five thousand dollars over the three years.
>
> Knowing what I do about your current situation, I would recommend Option One (whichever option makes sense for the customer) because your in-house team is strong enough to get up and running in that period of time and maintain the project themselves after the first year. (Whatever the reason is that you chose the option you did.) But, we both know it's not my money—it's yours.
>
> "So, let me ask you this—which option do you think works best for you?"

Then *hush*!

If you are new to this business, you have just asked for the sale. There is an old saying that "the first one that talks loses." I *hate* that saying. I'm not going to tell you to sweat the customer out. That is an old, tired strategy that will make you look less than professional if the prospect decides to "wait you out." Make this conversational *not* confrontational.

If you will take time to write yourself a script and practice, practice, practice until it becomes second nature to you, your sales will skyrocket!

Once again this should be planned *not* canned. Do not sound like a broken record. Be comfortable enough with the process that you can rattle it off just as if someone asked you your phone number. Make it so natural it just effortlessly.

Notice that when I talk about money I talk about it in a certain way. When I'm talking about the price I want it to sound small ($12,500=twelve-five). But, when I'm discussing savings or a discount I want it to sound *big* (three thousand dollars, five thousand dollars. *Use* the word "dollars").

But, what if they say no?

Please understand, the best answer that a salesperson can get when asking for a sale is "yes" or an affirmative response to move forward. The second best answer one can receive is "no." Yes, you did read that correctly. Of all the answers a prospect can give you when you ask for the sale the second best one to hear is, "No."

Because then—and only then, do you have something to work with. It is simply a balancing act. In fact, think of it as a scale; when the product or service you're offering means more to the prospect than the money it costs, you'll have a sale. Until then, you'll have objections. The prospect is constantly weighing the two in their mind. Understand this. Know what they're going through and how they are processing information. It will help you help them make an informed, sensible decision—and isn't that what we want?

I *love* to have a prospect tell me no. It is far better than the other possible objections of "I want to think about it, I'll get back to you," "I have to talk to whomever." Think about it, wouldn't you *love* to have them just tell you, no?

So, what do you say?

Here are a few tried and true questions you can have in your back pocket to use when needed. Memorize them. Know them. Have them handy!

- "Why do you say that?" (Wow. Simple, yet effective. Just ask. Why do they say, no?)
- "Really. I'm a bit surprised. Tell me more?" (Another very natural response. Use it. It works.)
- "What lead you to that decision?" (A variation of above, but it is designed to get the prospect talking about their thought process.)
- "Why?" (When all else fails . . . ask *why*?)

If you will commit these to memory and be sincere when delivering them, you will learn a lot about your prospects, customers, and yourself. Because, what they tell you will help you not only with them but with future clients as well.

I mentioned in the introduction of this book I had triple bypass heart surgery in May, 2009. I didn't have a heart attack—I got lucky: I caught it before it caught me. The reason I bring this up is because if someone had asked me on May 18, 2009, "Butch, would you like open heart surgery?" my response would've been, "I don't need it, don't want it, and can't afford it."

Sound familiar?

Those are probably the same objections we all hear every day of the week! Don't want it, don't need it, can't afford it.

After seeing the results of my heart catheterization, I changed my tune. Not only did I *need* it and I *wanted* it, I found a way to *afford* it, but I also wanted the best person I could find to do it!

I wanted an *expert*!

So, what changed? Simple. The information available to me was the only difference. On May 18, I had no idea there was a problem—on May 19, I was all in!

Do you realize that you have customers whose business is in as bad a condition as my heart was? And they need *you* to be the expert. They need you to show where the blockage is—to help them find ways to identify and solve problems.

You do that by asking questions and taking a genuine interest in their business. Then and only then do you become the expert they want to do business with.

Others may try to sell them something; while you're there to help them solve a problem. There is a *huge* difference.

I know it sometimes comes down to price. You're at the mercy of your stupidest competitor and there is always someone willing to give product away like they're going out of business.

We have all been guilty of thinking that if we just got the price down a little we'd have a deal. That can be a double-edged sword and the easy way out sometimes. Instead of cutting the price, think about adding value to your offer or offerings.

Preparing to Succeed

It's back to the scale we've talked about before. Instead of taking price off one side add value to the other. If you want to maintain a profit margin, you cannot give your product away. Besides giving it away takes no talent, skill, or ability.

Anybody can sell on price.

But, what can you add to the equation to make your price more appealing for your prospect? When you start to look at it in this manner, you sometimes have to be creative in what you add or in how you add it. Would better terms, financing, or other financial considerations solve the problem instead of lowering the price? Think creatively.

What other aspects of your agreement are negotiable? Make a list of everything that can be negotiated and put the price last. Get into the habit working every angle available before you even get into negotiating price.

Granted there are times where price is the only option—just make sure you've exhausted all others before you get out the price-chopper.

One bonus here is to add value with things that have a higher perceived value than their actual cost. For example if you are negotiating a deal on a landscaping job—offer to add two years of fertilizing and maintenance for the price of one year. Your *hard* cost in that is probably much lower than the perceived value.

It seems as if the price of everything we sell today is negotiable. Customers seldom expect to pay full price for whatever product you represent. If you're a commissioned salesperson, your ability to negotiate has a direct influence on your paycheck. And, even if you're not on commission, you're negotiation skills certainly have an impact on your company's bottom line.

Which brings me to an important point; not all sales are good sales. I know some people think more sales cures everything, but if you're losing money on every sale—the last thing you need to do is sell more!

Profitable sales are good sales.

Now, granted, one can argue that thin margins on certain key or large accounts produce buying power and other economies of scale that make smaller accounts more profitable and I agree with that 100%. But, as a sales professional you have to go into every relationship freely admitting your need to make a profit. I am continually surprised at some salespeople and their feelings of almost embarrassment about making a profit. Here's a newsflash for you; if you don't make a profit, you won't be around long.

So, in order to negotiate like a pro, I want you to remember one simple strategy; when you give something up, get something in return.

Have to cut your price? Then you should ask for shorter payment terms or other concessions that equate to a monetary difference to you.

If you have to give up anything from your side, you should ask for something from the customer's side in return.

How about payment terms, better delivery options, increased lead time, and other ways you can better use your assets? Can the customer take delivery at a later date allowing you to gain some efficiencies? Is the customer willing to take a floor model (with the same warranties and guarantees) as one in the box?

Simply put, what can you get that is of benefit to you and your company that is tangible?

Preparing to Succeed

Don't settle for the, "Well, I'll try to introduce you to somebody I know that knows somebody that might need your product next year," type deal. That's a whole lot of smoke.

Get something tangible that you can measure immediately.

Go into each relationship with this strategy: when they ask, you ask. You'll find the customer will have more respect for you as a professional and you'll have a more profitable customer, as well.

Be the expert. Make it your mission to help your prospects and customers uncover their pain points. Ask them, "How can I help *you*?" But, keep in mind they may not know they have a problem. You may have to be prepared to show them the blockage and show that you, the expert, has a solution.

Approach it like that and you will build yourself a nice little business and help a lot of people in the process!

One word of caution, you *must* come across with the right intent and attitude. You want them to see you as the expert—not tell them you are. It's like respect; you earn it you don't demand it. Take care not to come off as authoritative and talk down to your prospects. They should view you as the expert because of your mannerism, professionalism, and your actions.

But, we all know objections are going to come. No matter how good you are, the prospective customer is going to have objections.

As you get better and better these will become more natural, your closing percentage will increase, your anxiety will decrease, and your customer's will be happier. They found their expert.

I've given you some closing strategies for handling common objections. You need to identify the ten most common objections from your customers. Then identify techniques for closing those objections (you'll probably find solutions in the examples I've given you). Practice them, test them, and continue to refine them. By making this frequent review a habit, you will always be ready for the next sales call.

Remember, you need to know your ten most common objections by heart. You owe it to yourself to learn, practice, and be proficient at ways to overcome those ten.

ಳು

You don't close a sale, you open a relationship if you want to build a long-term, successful enterprise.
~Patricia Fripp

Know Your Customer

Habit #8
Spend an Extra Ten Minutes with Your Customer after the Sale

The sale is complete. The paperwork is done. You've gone through each step of the sales process and you have emerged with a new client. They're ready to take delivery or begin using your product or service.

When all is said and done, I want you to stop what you're doing and just get to know your new customer. Find out makes them tick. I know you went through the building rapport process in the beginning, but at that point you were on different sides of the aisle. Now, you're working toward a common goal; you're on the same team.

You will both be more relaxed and more comfortable around each other.

Let them talk. Talk about the sales process you just went through; don't be afraid to ask questions.

"Bob, so that I can continue to improve and serve my customer's, what was the deciding factor in you choosing us?"

Listen.

It is at this point you'll learn more about your customer than any other time in the relationship. The defenses and walls are down—you both sit on the same side of the table. Believe me, they want to help you.

They just made the decision to do business with you which means that they like you, they trust you, and they have confidence in you. Isn't that the type person you want to help?

Keep in mind I'm asking for an *extra* ten minutes—this is over and above what you would normally do in wrapping up the sale.

I submit to you that this time of afterglow is one of the best times to gather real, relevant information. You are going to learn things here you might never have the opportunity to find out about your client.

And at this point in the sales process, it's not necessarily about what their pain was today. You filled that need or you wouldn't have gotten the sale. Find out about other areas where they have issues—not that you are going to try to solve them today—but, file that information away for the future.

Don't get greedy. Get smarter.

Use this time to truly get to know your client as a person. Be sincere. Above all, listen. Actively. Listen intently. Just listen.

And, you'll begin to notice that things you learn in this *bonus* ten minutes will help you win more business in the future with other prospects. It will provide you with insight into how your prospect thinks, acts, and processes information. It will give you an unbelievable edge over your competition in understanding your customer's business.

Speaking of competition, this is a great time to learn about them and what their proposal was to your new customer. What can you learn about how they handled the sales process? What cost them the sale?

Anything you can learn is valuable information—and I cannot stress enough how much the easier the information is to gather after the sale is made.

So reframe these ten minutes in your mind. This is not the end; it's the beginning. Your job really starts now.

ಬ

**Worry about getting better;
bigger will take care of itself
~Gary Comer**

Keeping the Pipeline Full

Habit #9
Get Ten Referrals Every Month

As a professional salesperson, referrals can and should be the lifeblood of your business. Just look at any industry and I guarantee you the top 1% work almost exclusively by referral—they don't leave their business, livelihood, and income to chance.

The easiest sell any of us will ever make is to someone who was referred to us by a happy customer. Period. End of story.

I don't know who first said it; if I did I'd give them credit, but I have heard for years "You can manage what you can measure". Does that make sense? If you can measure it, you can manage it. So, you must have a list each month. If you will commit to tracking your referrals, you will immediately get more. If you just leave it to chance, it's not going to happen. There is work involved here. This may be simple stuff, but it's not always easy. You have to put in a little effort. You need to make it a habit of asking for referrals constantly. It must be part of your sales process. Perhaps it's even something you do in that *extra ten* minutes you spend with your customer? Oh…now, we're on to something.

There are other great ways to build your referral business to where customers are asking for you or your calendar is filled with appointments and you're not just the next salesperson "up"?

Here are three tips to get you started:

Be Referable: Yes, that's correct. If you want referrals you have to be referable. Are you handling your business like a true professional? Are you taking advantage of opportunities to show your current clients how fortunate they are to do business with you? I don't mean being cocky or arrogant, but being confident your customers are truly doing business with the expert in your field. This is a great place to start. You have to be someone that others want to do business with. You have to be referable.

Keep a Referral Log: If you leave this to chance you'll find yourself neglecting it. Create a referral log and commit to generating ten solid referral leads every month. Month in and month out. If you get fifteen this month that's great, but you still must get ten again next month. Don't rely on memory. Write them down. Know who referred you, where you were, what was said—get all the details. Simply by keeping track of your referrals you'll visually know where you are throughout the month. It will truly become an enjoyable process as you see that number—and your sales grow.

> *Give a referral:* One of the greatest ways to remind your customers to refer you is to refer them. Begin to think of ways to refer business to your customers and they will, in most cases, return the favor.

And then there is the big tip—ask. Yes, ask. It is that simple. My friend Hugh Liddle has what I think is a tremendous way to ask for referrals. When a customer comments on how well he's done or brag on him he always says, "Thank you. And don't keep me a secret! I work by referral and would love to help some of your friends." Think about that; don't keep me a secret! How simply beautiful is that?

The bottom line is this, if you want to be successful in sales, referrals must be a part of your business—and the longer you're in business they should become a larger part of it. You're closing ratio is much higher working with a referral than any other prospect.

One of the things I like to teach salespeople is to set aside part of their cold calling or prospecting time to call current clients to solicit referrals. However, do not make that the only reason you call. "Janet, I was going through my files, saw your name and wanted to call and check on you to see if there was anything I could do for you."

You may find an issue with a current customer by accident—and be able to take action. But, most likely you'll be met with a friendly, "I'm great. Thanks for checking on me." At that point you can turn the conversation toward referrals by asking, "Well, while I've got you, who do you know that I should be working with or calling on?"

Notice I didn't ask *if* Janet knew someone. I asked *who* she knew. This is a fundamental difference in how your client processes your request. You're now expecting an answer and you'll be much more likely to receive one—or more.

Most customers are happy to refer business to you—if you ask.

Once you get a referral, thank your client and always—always—follow up with them to let them know how the contact went. "Janet, I'm not going to take up much of your time, but wanted to let you know I called on the Petersons last week and it looks like they are going to become a client. I really appreciate you helping me build my business. It really means a lot. And if there is anything I can do for you, please let me know."

Now, once the Petersons become a customer, a handwritten (yes, handwritten) thank you card is in order for Janet. Do not take this for granted. Go out of your way to let your customers be a part of the process and they will actually begin to get into it. They will call *you* with referrals. It happens. Trust me.

Get them involved. Let them celebrate the wins with you because every time they do, it reinforces their decision to do business with you in the first place.

Finally, think about ways where you might help your customers grow their business.

So, how can you do this? If you're in retail sales, take a note from my friend Kevin who is the manager of a large paint store in Florida. Kevin recently shared with me that a lot of his customers are independent businessmen—and unfortunately, most are better painters than businessmen.

When they come in complaining about customers beating them up over price or competitors willing to shortcut a job and cheapen the service, Kevin has found a way to use empathy instead of sympathy while doing far more than just selling them paint. I'll let Kevin tell you about it:

> The first thing I suggest is that they stop trying to sell themselves on price. I learned long ago that if you try to compete on price, there are plenty other guys out there that are willing to beat you to the poor house.
>
> Since most of the pot and brush guys are better tradesmen than businessmen that of course brings up the question of how do you get the better customers. I'm trying to develop a new tip every month, but my first is to offer to return once a year for free touch-up. Call it a maintenance plan.
>
> I'm using that as a basis for several other marketing opportunities they can take advantage of. Not only does that get them back in front of the customer, but it also gives them a chance to sell other services, like pressure washing, to (their) customers. Plus they can go door to door to the neighbors, letting them know they are in the area and the services they offer.
>
> Then I suggest that if they have to take a low bid job, make sure they get a referral from that customer that can be used to sell the next job, preferably on video with the homeowner standing directly in front of their house."

I would venture to guess that Kevin sells a lot more paint than the average paint store, which ignores their customer's concerns. Kevin is not only showing his customers he cares, but he's offering them genuine, creative ideas to improve their business. Now that is being professional!

Do you think Kevin gets referrals? You bet! He's first being referable. He's building his business and his customer's business.

In his book, *Get More Referrals Now*, author Bill Cates suggests referrals should be your primary source of new business and goes on to say, "The way of the world is meeting people through other people, and the referral is the warm way to get into people's lives."

Is it easy? No. But, over time it becomes much, much easier because it becomes part of what you do; not something you *have* to do. And, how far away can ten referrals be from ten new clients?

ଔ

Profit in a business comes from repeat customers, customers that brag about your project or service, and that bring friends with them.
~W. Edwards Deming

Never Stop Learning and Growing

Habit #10
Invest Ten Percent of Your Income in Marketing Yourself and in Personal Development

We've covered nine habits designed to make you a leader in your industry. Habits that if followed, can and will allow you to experience explosive growth in your life and career. But, that's not enough. To really experience the Power of Ten—to hit that superstar level, you must continually invest in *you*.

This is not just about developing your skills (we'll talk about those in a bit), but this is marketing yourself as the expert we've been discussing.

Marketing Yourself

Working with salespeople, I've found more than a few of them to be very good at selling everything—except themselves. I'm not talking about selling themselves in the process of selling their product, but in actually marketing themselves and taking on the role of the go-to person for their field. Someone has to be that person. Why not you?

If I were to ask, "Why should I buy from you?" what would be the answer? What would you say? Why are you better than your competition or every other person who is selling your product or service?

If you don't have an answer, you need one. You need a *why*. That *why* is your USP (unique selling proposition or unique selling position) and it's the difference between you and your competition. It is, in essence, the reason others should choose you over everyone else who does what you do.

What makes you special? What makes you unique? What sets you apart? If you are drawing a blank, that's okay. Fortunately, it's a solvable problem. Just take a little time and flesh out the answer. Work with other salespeople or your manager if you have to and come up with at least one thing that separates you from the competition.

Why should I buy from you? It could be something tangible like a better warranty, a money back guarantee, the materials you use in the manufacturing of your product, your delivery time, turnaround time, or any number of different things. It could be even be awards you've won or things you've accomplished in your career. Or, it could be something intangible. It could simply be you. Yes, you. Your ability and commitment to take care of your customer and their needs after the sale.

I've worked with businesses where everyone sold the same product for about the same price and provided similar services. How are you going to differentiate yourself there? The difference has to be you. This is where your confidence, commitment, and attitude comes in. Sell the customer on your ability to handle their account personally and professionally and make sure they are happy for many years to come.

Never Stop Learning and Growing

In my career, I used tell prospects all the time, "You know we all sell about the same thing for about the same price but there's one thing that my company has that the competition can never duplicate." This would always get me a, "What?"

"Me. Me along with my desire and commitment to make sure you are happy and for you to know that no matter what happens, Butch is going to take care of it. Are we going to make mistakes? Sure, but there is nobody out there who is going to work harder to take care of you and make sure you're able to serve your customers." You know what? Many times that is much more important than an extended warranty or a better guarantee.

Don't be afraid to be unique. Rise to the challenge, build your own brand. Build the brand of you. Are you promoting yourself as something special and first in your field? Do clients in your industry think of you first? They should. When you have successfully built the brand that is you, you obtain that top-of-mind awareness when a client or potential client needs your product or services.

But, here's something that might surprise you. You have a personal brand already, whether you control it or not. Think about that. Your actions, your character, your reputation, and how you are perceived in the marketplace is establishing a pattern—it's establishing a brand. You should control it instead of allowing others to do so. You must be proactive instead of reactive.

In order to take control of it you must consistently deliver, time and time again earning a reputation as someone who others want to do business with. It doesn't happen overnight. It is a process that takes time.

But you have to start now. And you have to start with all the pieces. Do your sales materials—from your business cards to customer forms—scream professionalism? They should. Do you market yourself as much as your product? Rome wasn't built in a day and you won't establish your brand by tomorrow. But, you have to be conscious of it and at least working to control it and build it into what you want it to be.

So, how to you do that? First take every opportunity to position yourself in that light; speak at events, write a newsletter, be a resource regarding your industry for news media, set up a blog, position yourself as the person in your industry. You should be like the old E.F. Hutton television commercials, "When you talk, people listen."

Don't be afraid to be creative and have fun with your brand. Nobody said success comes to the most serious person. You must be memorable. Be different. Stand out. If your industry is like most it won't take a lot to stand out and for you to be the leader.

It's your brand. Build it and they will come!

Investing In Yourself

I heard Zig Ziglar say one time, "You are where you are today because of what has gone into your mind." Think about that; the information, education, and all other input that has fueled your brain has led you to right where you are today. Where will you be tomorrow? If you don't like where you are or want to change where you are, the best way to do that is to change what goes into your mind. Change your thoughts and you can change your world.

We live in a world that is moving at a record pace and if you're going to change your place in it, you must do so in a manner like never before.

Never Stop Learning and Growing

It starts with the positive, professional, motivational material you feed yourself. So, where will you be tomorrow? Will you be right where you are today? Will you be better off or not in as good a position? Finding inspirational messages that motivate and focus you will provide a vehicle to shift your thoughts; change your thoughts and you can change your world.

Another way to change your world is to create a clear vision of the world that you want. Try this exercise. I want you to write down today's date— not just the month and day but add the year as one year from today—365 days away.

Now, ask yourself these five questions:

1. Where will I be on this date in _____?
2. What will I have accomplished?
3. What will I have learned?
4. What skills will I have improved?
5. What goals will I have achieved?

The answer to each of those questions is within reach. For the answer to each of these questions is up to you and you alone. You have the power and the time to make significant changes in your business and your life within the next 365 days. Here's how.

Step One—Write down what you want the answer to be to each of the questions above.

As you write them, do so as if they've already occurred—as if you're reading them in the present tense next year on this date. For example, the first one could be "I am the top salesperson in my company. I'm financially, spiritually, emotionally, and physically healthy with a family that I adore and that loves me very much."

Wow! How would you like to be *there* a year from now? Guess what? You can be. Again, it's completely up to you.

Step Two—Take each of these five statements (they are not goals) and post them where you can see them each day at least once without having to look for them.

(Somewhere that they'll find you!)

Step Three—Make time to read these affirmations aloud every day for the next year.

As you do, think about what it is going to take to make that statement true. What do you need to do today so that you can actually make that statement a fact next year? Do it daily (aloud) without fail.

Step Four—Before you go to bed each night, look at this list one more time quietly.

Study it. Let it sink in to your brain. Try to make yourself dream about the fact that you've already achieved and accomplished the things on this list. See it in your mind's eye.

Step Five—Make the commitment today that nothing will prohibit you from making these statements factual by next year.

Make the commitment. Decide now. We've talked about investing in something truly worthwhile—you. There is no better investment anywhere on this planet. No stock. No bond. Nothing. You must invest in the future that you want.

Now, go out there and make it happen. Each day you'll chip away at it. Each day will move you a little closer to the end result.

If you will do this, I can tell you right now where you'll be in a year without a doubt! But, do not get discouraged. This is a journey of 365 days. If part of your list is to lose weight or get in shape, understand that you aren't going to lose twenty pounds by tomorrow morning. At the same time, you aren't going to achieve the other things you want to accomplish in that amount of time either. But, commit to the process and enjoy the ride. It's going to be a great year for you!

Another way to invest in yourself is by improving your skills, your knowledge, and your expertise. From podcasts on your mobile phone to listening to materials through a set of ear buds during your lunch hour—you *do* have time to put more information into your brain. Don't use the excuse that you don't have time.

I'm going to give you a secret—the one key—the missing link, if you will—to sales success. I am going to share with you something that salespeople have sought for decades. Many have written books pondering the difference between the average salesperson and those who experience an extraordinary amount of success. And, right here today I'm going to impart to you how you become that superstar and achieve that level of not just success, but *ultra*-success. Are you ready? Really, are you ready?

Write this down—*find the most successful person in your industry and do what they do*. Ta Da! That's it. That's the big secret. Yes, that's the key. I will wager that you will find they spend an inordinate amount of time improving themselves. Reading, writing, practicing—whatever it takes to be better at what they do. There is no more magic than that.

But, therein lies the rub. Most people, in fact the vast majority, have no interest in finding out what that person is doing, much less doing it, too. Everyone wants a pretty baby but nobody wants the labor pain. And, you can't have one without the other.

Once you find that top performer and observe them, you can bet they are reading books (or blogs or other good material), studying their craft, honing their skills, learning new closes and doing all those things that nobody else wants to do. They work all day on Friday. They get to work early and don't waste their selling hours on things that don't produce sales. They've refined their business to an art.

And, the good news is you can too! But, will you?

Another thing you will find is that virtually every top performer loves to share their success strategies with someone who is truly interested in improving their skills. I believe one of the main ingredients in those successful people is the desire to help others. So, as you start to grow and achieve more, I want you to share those same secrets with someone else. It will do you both a world of good.

We've heard the saying, "Practice makes perfect" since we were children. We heard it about sports, about music, about school—really about anything that our parents or others wanted to see us improve. And, for the most part it's correct.

I know, I know. Some have revised it to say, "Perfect practice makes perfect." And I agree with that to an extent. It's my belief that just because you aren't perfect doesn't mean you shouldn't practice. In fact, that's the reason you should in the first place. Again, an investment in yourself could mean investing in practice—investing time in working to get better at what you do.

I'm asking you to practice your job. I mean really practice. Practice meeting and greeting prospective customers. Practice answering objections and asking good questions. Practice making new contacts, asking for the sale, and generating referrals.

Practice making a better you. Why would you not do this? If you had the same hours to practice your golf game or practice tennis or whatever wouldn't you rather have a better you?

Never Stop Learning and Growing

When I talk about investing in yourself, I'm not only talking about money I'm also talking about time. If you spent hours learning to bend your knees and keep your glove on the ground for Little League, why would you not put in hours of practice to hone your craft that makes you a living? Do you think doctors or attorneys or dentists or other professions continually learn and practice? What about airline pilots? Many of them are tested twice a year and if they don't pass, they don't work. (I think we can all agree with that.) So, why aren't you devoting a number of hours each week to studying and practicing the art of sales? Read books, role play with a manager or colleague, attend seminars or webinars, or just look into a mirror and work on a part of your presentation. You aren't as good as you can be—yet. So, keep practicing.

One of the best ways I've found to practice is to role play with another salesperson while a manager, coach or another salesperson looks on. Let them take notes and critique. Practice until you get it right. And, the best part is all three of the participants end up learning something. Yes, even the old manager who knows everything. How do I know this? Well, I hope you've learned something from this book. But, I can assure you that I learned far more in the process of writing it and putting it together than you could ever get by reading it.

I recently received an email newsletter from a well-respected author and the title was *Failure Is an Option*. I'm not really sure what he was trying to accomplish with that title, maybe just the shock-effect, but to me failure is not an option. It never is for me. And it's only an option for you if you allow it to be. If I've imparted anything to you within these pages, I hope it is that you are in complete control of your career, your success, and your future.

You only fail if you quit, right? So, as long as you're still in the game and there's time on the clock—you haven't lost. You haven't failed. But, let's say you do lose a deal or have a bad month in your business. Is that "failure"? I don't think so. If I had to define failure it would be this: Having a less than successful experience from which you learned nothing.

If you gain knowledge or experience even if you don't succeed, you don't fail—at least not in my eyes. The opposite of success is not failure. The opposite of success is quitting. Whether you're in sales or operate your own small business—as long as you don't throw up your hands and quit—you are still in the game.

Use these strategies to market and invest in yourself. Create a budget and allocate 10% of your income to marketing, motivational materials, and improving your skills and knowledge. But, also devote your time to visualizing the world you want, modeling the behavior of successful people, and practicing your craft.

I believe you are a worthwhile investment.

ಞ

**An investment in knowledge
pays the best interest.
~Benjamin Franklin**

Epilogue

Some of you who are reading this are old enough to remember the 1965 hit, "What The World Needs Now Is Love." For those of us who've heard the song (it was released the year I was born), it was fitting of the turbulent times in the country, with civil rights and foreign wars dominating the headlines.

Almost fifty years later as of this writing, I ask myself, "What does the world need now? What is it that we are we really in desperate need of?"

In my opinion, it's leaders. We need leaders; leaders in business, leaders in civic organizations, leaders in our communities, leaders in our schools, leaders in our churches.

We need leaders. Perhaps we need them now more than ever. Webster defines a leader as, "Someone who leads; to guide on a way especially by going in advance." That's what we need—leaders; leaders to go on ahead of everyone else and let everyone know what can be accomplished if we all work together. Leaders who set examples and aren't afraid to model them. Leaders who are willing to go against the mainstream or popular notion of what can and cannot be accomplished—those are real leaders.

Are you ready to be a leader? You can start right where you are today. Commit to being a leader in your home, your job, your community and go from there.

The great part about being a leader is that you can literally begin any time anywhere, because you simply lead by example. Decide today that you're going to become a leader in your profession hold nothing back.

One of my life's missions is to break the mold of the stereotypical salesman. To this day in some contexts "salesman" is almost a dirty word and that really bothers me. I mean it *really* bothers me.

I'm proud to tell people I am a salesman! I love it. I *live* it! But, I do it professionally.

The problem is that an image of a *huckster* still permeates some people's vision of salespeople. But, that can be changed; one person, one sale, one contact at a time. And it is up to us; the *professional* salespeople that make an honest living and genuinely love our business and take pride in taking care of our customers.

So, what can you do to help break that mold? What can you do to change people's perception? Very simply, be professional at all times—in your dress, your manners, your actions, your reactions, and in your handling of contacts, prospects and customers.

Make it a point to exude professionalism. Go out of your way to rise above what people think you should be.

Treat everyone you meet professionally. It has been well documented that at the time Sam Walton was the richest man in America, he could be seen driving around Bentonville, Arkansas in an old pickup truck and well-worn clothes. Nobody would've believed he was worth billions. Never forget that.

Epilogue

Take pride in your work. I know this is a given, but really make it a point to be proud of what you do, who you are, and the products you represent.

Stand up for the profession. If you see or hear anything around your workplace that contributes to the negative stereotypes, I believe you have the ability and responsibility to do something about it or at least bring it to a manager's attention. That sort of poison can cost *you* business and there's no place for it.

Treat those that don't buy from you just as well as you do those that do. I am going to assume you treat your customer's well. But, I'm going to challenge you to treat the *nos* as well as the *yeses*. It will make you stronger and more professional over time.

Smile. Yes, smile. Enjoy what you do. If you aren't having fun going to work, do yourself and everyone else a favor and do something else. Life is too short.

You should treat the profession of a salesperson like you would that of a doctor, dentist, or any other highly paid professional. You deserve it. Once you begin to feel that way, you'll conduct yourself that way. You are part of the greatest profession on earth—be proud of it!

Together we can break that mold. But, I need *your* help!

Appendix

Tools for Creating the Habits of Sales Superstars

Use the following links to download forms that will allow you to begin creating habits immediately.

Habit 1
Weekly New Contact Form
http://butchbellah.com/wp-content/uploads/2014/05/Copy-of-Habit-1-Ten-New-Contacts-Per-Week.pdf

Habit 2
Top Ten List
http://butchbellah.com/wp-content/uploads/2014/05/Copy-of-Habit-2-Top-Ten-List.pdf

Habit 4
My Goals
http://butchbellah.com/wp-content/uploads/2014/05/Copy-of-Habit-4-Goals-Form.pdf

Habit 5
Monthly New Prospect Form
http://butchbellah.com/wp-content/uploads/2014/05/Copy-of-Habit-5-Ten-New-Prospects-Per-Month.pdf

Habit 6
Current/Lost Customer Contact Log
http://butchbellah.com/wp-content/uploads/2014/05/Copy-of-Habit-6-Current-or-Lost-Customer-Log.pdf

Habit 9
Referral Log
http://butchbellah.com/wp-content/uploads/2014/05/Copy-of-Habit-9-Referral-Log.pdf

About the Author

Butch Bellah is owner of B2 Training & Development where he is a speaker, sales trainer, and author. He has more than twenty-five years of hands-on experience in sales, sales management, and sales training. Today he works with companies and individuals to help them get more appointments, land more business, and retain more customers—all while focused on bottom line profits. He is an accomplished speaker where he draws on his more than ten years of experience as a professional stand-up comedian.

He was recently named one of the Top 50 Sales Experts and one of the Top 100 Business Coaches to follow on Twitter.

In May 2009, he underwent triple bypass heart surgery at forty-three and used the experience to change his life and the lives of others. On Thanksgiving Day 2009, 190 days after his surgery,

Butch ran his first 5K in 36:45 minutes. In 2013, he ran twenty-two 5Ks (with a PR of 31:41), a 10K, and two half marathons.

In his spare time he enjoys smooth jazz, 80s music, and writing.

He splits his time between Dallas, Texas and his home in Lafayette, Louisiana. He and his wife Angie have three children, two dogs, and three grand dogs.

Praise for

The Ten Essential Habits of Sales Superstars

The Ten Essential Habits of Sales Super Stars: Plugging into the Power of Ten is a terrific "handbook" of practical, bare-bones sales training. It's brief but thorough, and easy to understand and apply. As Dad would say, "We don't always need to be told, but we often need to be reminded." Kudos to Butch Bellah!
—Tom Ziglar
President/CEO, Ziglar, Inc.

☙

Butch Bellah packs a lot of rock-solid advice into this little book. Apply just one habit and your sales will increase; apply more and you'll get 10x the results.
—Jill Konrath
Author of *Agile Selling* and *Snap Selling*

☙

The Ten Essential Habits of Sales Superstars is just that—essential. It should be part of every salesperson's library and arsenal. Read it. Learn it. Use it. When it comes to sales books, this one should make the Top Ten List.
—Robert Terson
Best-Selling Author of *Selling Fearlessly: A Master Salesman's Secrets for the One-Call-Close Salesperson*

Finally a "go to" book for the salesperson who thinks about what they need to do but fails to do it. Butch Bellah lays out 10 succinct steps to make you more successful as a salesperson.

    —Mark Hunter
     The Sales Hunter—Top 50 Most Influential
     Sales & Marketing Leaders
     Best-Selling Author of *High-Profit Selling*

~

Butch Bellah is a sales leader that speaks from the heart and has the experience to back it up. In *Ten Essential Habits of Sales Superstars*, Butch packs 25 years of road-tested sales tools, techniques and strategies to help both the new and experienced seller not only achieve greater success, but also enjoy the journey. It is an insightful roadmap for changing your habits and thus, changing your results. It provides specific direction for challenges like, getting past gatekeepers, filling your pipeline or turning a *suspect* into a qualified *prospect*. I am personally going to adopt Butch's advice to create a Top Ten List and ask myself each day, "what can I do to move each relationship forward?"

    —Julie Hansen
     Sales Trainer and Founder, Performance Sales
     and Training

~

Butch Bellah, sales coach extraordinaire, has hit a total home run with his new book *The Ten Essential Habits of Sales Superstars*. It's an incredible start up manual for anyone embarking on a sales career, and there are hundreds of valuable reminders for us veteran salespeople who aren't doing the things that made us successful to start with! No wonder Butch Bellah is one of the most awesome salespeople and sales coaches I've ever seen. And now he's revealed how YOU can do it too!

    —Hugh Liddle
     THE Sales Wizard at Red Cap Sales Coaching

I'M
T.O.U.G.H

Tackling Obstacles and
Unleashing God's Hope

A 60 Day Devotional Designed to Firmly
Establish You Using Simple Biblical Principles

INDIA REAVES

DMI PUBLISHING HOUSE
HAMPTON

Copyright © 2014 - India Reaves

All rights reserved. This book is protected by the copyright laws of the United States of America. This book may not be copied or reprinted for commercial gain or profit. The use of quotations or occasional page copying for personal or group study is permitted and encouraged. Permission will be granted upon request.

Unless otherwise identified, Scripture quotations are from the King James Version. Copyright © 1982 by Thomas Nelson, Inc. Used by permission. All rights reserved. Scripture quotations marked NLT are taken from the Holy Bible, New Living Translation, copyright ©1996, 2004, 2007 by Tyndale House Foundation. Used by permission of Tyndale House Publishers, Inc., Carol Stream, Illinois 60188. All rights reserved. Scripture quotations marked The Message are taken from THE MESSAGE. Copyright © by Eugene H. Peterson 1993, 1994, 1995, 1996, 2000, 2001, 2002. Used by permission of Tyndale House Publishers, Inc. Emphasis within Scripture is the author's own.

Take note that the name satan and related names are not capitalized. We choose not to acknowledge him, even to the point of violating grammatical rules.

Cover Design: Tia W. Cooke
Author Photo: Still Shots Photography

Library of Congress Control Number: 2014938378
ISBN 978-0-6922-0263-0

DMI Publishing House
(a division of Dominion Media International, LLC)
P. O. Box 101
Windsor, VA 23487
www.dominionmediainternational.com

Printed in the United States of America.

Dedication

This book is dedicated to two immensely instrumental people in my life.

The first being my late mother, Kathy L. Reaves. In the 19 years that I had you here on earth, you gave me all that you had and I am who I am because you were who you were. Because of you, I am a God-fearing woman, a dreamer, a visionary, a leader, a true friend, a loving heart, a sister to many, a hug giver, a listening ear, a world changer, a vanguard woman, a surrogate, a nurturer, a sweet spirit, a go getter, a beacon of self-sufficiency, a confidence breeder, and an all-around authentic person. All of these are characteristics you taught me, not by the words from your mouth, but by the life you lived. In 19 years, you prepared me and gave me everything I needed to make it without you physically being here, and for that I am forever grateful. It is my desire that the summation of my life until this point is something that you are beyond proud of. Thank you for simply being you, the absolute best mother in the whole, entire world. I love you always K. Lo!

To the late great Reverend Philemon A. Samuels – my first Pastor – but most importantly my spiritual father. You recognized the anointing on my life when I was 5 years old. Once you recognized it, you nurtured it, tilled it, cultivated it, called it forth, and allowed me to operate in it. Your teachings were impeccable. Your integrity was uncompromising. Your vision was years beyond the times. Your love was gracious. Your ability to forgive was unrivaled. Your leadership was incomparable. Your ministry was authentic. Your heart was genuine. You were such an instrumental piece to the development of my spiritual man. I thank God for the opportunity to have sat under your leadership for 21 years. Although you are not physically here to bear witness to all that God is doing in my life, I know without a shadow of a doubt that you are standing over the banister of Heaven with the biggest smile on your face. All that you prayed over me, all that you spoke into me, all that you pulled out of me, is coming to fruition at this very moment. So I thank you for being the visionary, the covering, and the father that you were. I love you and appreciate you more than you will ever know! Love Babydoll!

Acknowledgements

I must first honor, acknowledge, and express my gratitude to God. Without Him I am nothing, I have nothing, and I could be nothing. Acts 17:28 says it perfectly, "For in Him we live and move and have our being, as also some of your own poets have said, 'For we are also His offspring." Thank you for the calling, thank you for the anointing, thank you for the vision, and thank you for the grace to carry it out!

I would like to thank my grandmother, Mildred R. Griffin. Granny, not by the words from your mouth, but through your lifestyle, you've taught me if you take care of what God loves, and that's His people, He will always take care of you. Your selflessness and your willingness to always serve are priceless lessons for which I am forever grateful. Your fight for the cause of equality in education inspired me to become an educator. Your perseverance encouraged me to never give up. Your work ethic motivates me to always give my best. Thank you for your love, your support, and most importantly your prayers. I know without a shadow of a doubt that I have a praying grandmother. I love you always.

Thank you to my Pastor, Gloria M. Samuels. You have pastored me for the past 25 years and the fact that I can say that is extremely rare. Your presence in my life is incomparable. Thank you for believing in and trusting the God in me, even when I couldn't. Thank you for never throwing in the towel concerning me. I'm grateful for every pinch, for every rebuke, for every fussing out and, for every parenting moment. I truly understand that it was all done because you saw what I couldn't see in myself, and refused to allow me to throw it away. I never understood why you rode me so hard until now. It was for this very moment and the many moments to come. I understand that your chastisement was always accompanied by an undergirding of love. You are authentic in every area of your life. You genuinely love what God loves. You are unapologetic in your bold approach to ministry. You are a warrior in the Body of Christ. You are a mother of Zion. Thank you for your prayers, your intercession, your parenting, your pastoring, and your covering. I am forever grateful. I love and appreciate you more than you will ever know.

To my family, the Reaves' the Griffin's, and the Roseboro's, I would like to thank each and every one of you for your consistent support. You all continuously held my arms up and pushed me forward. You prayed with and for me. There are no words that I could ever use that would accurately convey my gratitude. You have been with me through the most trying times of my life and I am beyond grateful. Each of you has an irreplaceable space in my heart. To my little brothers, Jordan Griffin and Michael Anthony Taylor, I pray that my life is a positive example for you to follow. I hope this book shows you that nothing is impossible if you believe! To the best first cousins ever, Porcia Reaves and Jamita Griffin, you ladies are much more than cousins. You are my sisters. Thank you both for a lifetime of support, encouragement, and sisterhood that we've shared. I love you all.

I would like to thank ALL of my friends and extended family. There are too many of you to name, but I am beyond blessed to have you all doing "LIFE" with me. You all are much more than friends, but more like family. God allowed me to experience His perfect favor for me when He allowed our paths to cross. We've been ratchet together, we've gotten into the most unsavory situations together, we've partied and ran the streets together, we've argued, we've made up, and now we are serving Christ together. Simply put, from one extreme to the other, my friends and extended family have been such an intricate part of my life and I want to say thank you from the bottom of my heart. I love you all!

To my family at Great Commission Community Church, Incorporated, you are the BEST CHURCH IN THE WHOLE WIDE WORLD. So much more than church members, you all are definitely my family. Thank you all for your unceasing encouragement and support. Thank you all for believing in me. Thank you for allowing me to serve you. Thank you for allowing me to present Solomon's Corner every Sunday for the past year and a half. Those Solomon's Corner messages have now evolved into I'm T.O.U.G.H! To Dr. Valderia Raynor, thank you for trusting and believing in me to carry out this assignment. You trusted me in what I couldn't and I am grateful. I am so blessed to be a part of such a dynamic, vision oriented, people loving, integrity filled, and authentic ministry! Great Commission, you all are second to none! I love you all so much…muahhhh!

I want to thank my students, both past and present. You guys have given me more than I could have ever imagined. In the 6 years that God has entrusted me with young people, you have changed my life in ways that I never thought possible. You have pulled out parts of me that I never even thought existed. You have caused me to always put my best foot forward, because that is what you all deserved. I don't take it lightly that God chose me for you and He chose you for me! You have no idea how much you all have encouraged me. Although I am not a mother in the natural, you have given me the opportunity to understand parenting – the good, the bad, the ugly, and the unconditional and unlimited love a mother has for her children and the desire to want better for you than you even know that you want for yourself. I look forward to seeing you all transform into world changing, history making, and ground-breaking young adults! I appreciate you all more than you will ever know. From Yellowjackets to Mustangs, Ms. Reaves loves you!

I want to thank my best friend, my sister, and my manager, Marian Wilkins. For the past 15 years you have been an absolutely amazing friend. We've literally grown up together. Who would have ever thought that we being placed in a group to work together in 10th grade would have turned into a life-long friendship? There is no one that I could trust more to manage, guard, and protect this project than you. Your heart is genuine, your friendship is real, your work ethic is impeccable, and your commitment is unparalleled. You push me and you inspire me. I'm so excited to take this journey with you! I love you Nae!

To my dear friend, my editor, and my publisher, Tia W. Cooke, where do I start? Thank you for allowing God to use you to present this life-changing opportunity before me. I wasn't looking for it, nor was I expecting it, but God had it all planned. There will never be enough words in my vocabulary that could ever express my gratitude for your place in my life. Thank you for being the midwife to this baby that is being birthed out of me. Your gifting, your talent, your anointing is unmatched. You are such a blessing to the entire Body of Christ. Thank you for believing in what God has placed inside of me. Thank you for fussing, preaching, pushing, encouraging, and guiding me through this process. I love you TT!

And finally, to LIFE, thank you! At times you tried to break me. You occasionally threw fiery darts at me. You often times dished out low blows. You attempted to knock me down. You broke my heart. You made me cry. You weren't always fair. You didn't show much mercy. You aimed to make me quit. But little did you know, your attempts to break me made me stronger. Your darts taught me agility. Your low blows made me tougher. Your knock downs instilled bounce back in me. Your heartbreak showed me God's healing power. Your tears made me appreciate joy. Your unfairness reminded me that the Lord is my true justifier. Your lack of mercy made me trust God even more. Your aims to make me quit made me hold on even longer. So yes, I have to say thank you.

It is on the shoulders of giants that I am here today. I will never forget to acknowledge those who have grabbed my hand, held my arms up, pushed me forward, or put me on their backs to make sure that I ended up here. I love all of you!

India

Contents

Foreword		15
Day 1	The Opportunity to Dream Again	17
Day 2	The Willow Tree Parable	21
Day 3	First Comes Humility, then Comes Honor	23
Day 4	Obedience is Always Better than Sacrifice	25
Day 5	Moving Forward is Too Risky, but Going Back is Too Costly	27
Day 6	Change Your Mind	31
Day 7	Extreme Makeover	33
Day 8	The Blessedness in Brokeness	35
Day 9	I've Got Your Back	39
Day 10	All Faith, No Fear	43
Day 11	Go Get 'Em Soldier	45
Day 12	From Feces to Fertilizer	47
Day 13	Love Without Limits	49
Day 14	Check Your Motives	51
Day 15	There is No Need For Competition in the Body of Christ	53
Day 16	No Compromising	55
Day 17	I Am What You See	57
Day 18	Crucifying the Spirit of the Waster	59
Day 19	What are You Doing With Your Talents?	61
Day 20	What I Learned From a Sea Turtle	65
Day 21	First Things First: A Lesson in Prioritizing	67
Day 22	To Get Abundance, Mediocrity Must Die	69
Day 23	Kill the Root, Kill the Fruit	71
Day 24	Real versus Fake: Developing Authentic Faith	75
Day 25	I Shall Not Be Moved	77
Day 26	Don't Miss Your Exit	79
Day 27	Stay Focused	81
Day 28	So What are You Saying?	83
Day 29	Just a Reminder	85

Day 30	Your Influence	89
Day 31	From Ratchet to Righteous	91
Day 32	Just Forget About It	93
Day 33	It May Have Been Your Desire, But it Wasn't Your Destiny	95
Day 34	Moving From Emotional Tribulation to Emotional Victory	99
Day 35	They Will Follow Your Example Before They Follow Your Instruction	101
Day 36	From a Faith Talker to a Faith Walker	103
Day 37	Shedding Dead Weight	105
Day 38	The Changing of the Seasons	107
Day 39	Don't Settle for an Ishmael When God Promised You an Isaac	111
Day 40	Great Things Start Small	113
Day 41	A Closed Mouth Won't Get Fed	117
Day 42	Opportunity Is Knocking	119
Day 43	Lord Help My Disbelief	121
Day 44	Don't Let Your Feelings Make You Forget	125
Day 45	From Tragedy to Triumph	129
Day 46	Salt and Light	131
Day 47	A Lesson From A Snowflake	133
Day 48	One Man's Trash is Another Man's Treasure	137
Day 49	You Can't Access the Promise Without Following the Instruction	139
Day 50	Footprints versus Fossils	141
Day 51	Don't Let the Fire Die	143
Day 52	No Shortcuts	145
Day 53	Keep Your Eyes on the Prize	149
Day 54	Surprise or Not	151
Day 55	His Yoke is Easy	153
Day 56	What's on Your Mind?	157
Day 57	The Man in the Mirror	159
Day 58	It was a Setup	163
Day 59	Please Don't Let Me Fall	167
Day 60	It Will Cost You Everything	169

Foreword

I am so honored to share in this foreword how very proud I am of the author. Many years ago – at least 25 – I had the distinct honor of meeting this five year old bubbly child that sang in the senior choir that only rendered hymns on Sunday morning worship services. I thought it odd that she attended choir rehearsal with her great aunt. Even odder was the fact that she actually sang with them and enjoyed it! I noticed in her growing up that she would always want you to ask her, "What do you want to be when you grow up." Trust me when I tell you I have heard it all, but teacher, judge, and preacher always stood out. This child always had dreams of becoming great no matter what her ambitions were. She would always display greatness.

As India entered into her teen years, it became challenging for us to communicate effectively. Prior to her becoming a teenager we could talk about everything, but as is normal for teens, our level of communication diminished. I was her First Lady and she no longer felt that she could tell me everything. It became clear that her path to ministry – even life – was being tested beyond measure. India would always test the boundaries. As much as the enemy was trying to destroy, discourage, disgrace and even get her to disown God, He had a plan. The plan included India as an educator, touching the lives of young people. I remember at six years old, she would say, "One day I am going to help young people like you." Well here she is at this moment with the opportunity to share her story of hope, courage, strength, failures, success, and even insecurities. This is all possible because she learned one of the best lessons she could ever learn. That lesson is obeying and trusting

God, our Creator. He will always help you to see a clearer picture of who you really are.

I have the distinction of pastoring a five year old little girl that has grown up to be a fine, young woman. The correction and rebuking was necessary. The crying, stomping, talking back under her breath, rebellion, and even threats could not take away or discredit the greatness in her. Hear the words in this devotional and you will know the journey of India Reaves thus far. I pray that it will bless you the way it has blessed our church family, Great Commission Community Church, Inc. on Sunday Mornings during the presentation of Solomon's Corner. Perhaps you will cry, laugh, become angry, smile, have mixed feelings or overwhelming emotions reading this book. However, it will leave you embracing and knowing that hope is worth holding out for. Enjoy *I'm T.O.U.G.H.*!

Pastor Gloria M. Samuels
Senior Pastor, *Great Commission Community Church, Inc.*

Day 1

THE OPPORTUNITY TO DREAM AGAIN

Joel 2:25-28 (NLT)
> The Lord says, "I will give you back what you lost to the swarming locusts, the hopping locusts, the stripping locusts, and the cutting locusts. It was I who sent this great destroying army against you. Once again you will have all the food you want, and you will praise the Lord your God, who does these miracles for you. Never again will my people be disgraced. Then you will know that I am among my people Israel, that I am the Lord your God, and there is no other. Never again will my people be disgraced. "Then, after doing all those things, I will pour out my Spirit upon all people. Your sons and daughters will prophesy. Your old men will dream dreams, and your young men will see visions.

Have you ever been in a place where you felt like you had wasted time? Have you ever felt like you missed a once in a lifetime opportunity because of your own foolishness, fear, lack, or slothfulness? Have you ever been in a place where you no longer dreamed – a place where you became content in just getting by? Has the thought of what could have been or if only I had, ever crossed your mind? If so, this is for you.

During the 1920's, the well-known African-American poet Langston Hughes asked a prolific question in one of his most notable pieces of work. His question was, "What happens to a dream deferred?" Hughes is questioning what becomes of a dream that is delayed, tossed aside, or obstructed by internal or external forces.

So today I present this same question to you. What has happened to your dream that was deferred? Have setbacks, insecurities, self-doubt, foolish mistakes, or wasted time caused you to put those God-given, obtainable dreams on the back burner? Are you in a constant state of "I should have," or "I could have," or "If only I had the chance to do it over again?" Have you been pushed or pulled so far away from your goals and aspirations that the mere thought of you accomplishing them now is somewhat unrealistic? Has the torch that the dreamer in you bears been extinguished by the storms and winds that life has dealt you? If so, I have some good news!

The amazing thing about the God we serve is that He is the ultimate restorer of time! He can breathe life back into the dreams that He placed down inside of you that you thought had died! If a business is what you dreamed, start it! If a book is what you desire, write it! If it's an album that's in your heart, record it! If it's a marathon that you want to run, train for it! If it's a weight goal you want to obtain, work for it! If it's a screenplay that is in your spirit, write and cast it. If it's debt free that you are seeking, get it! If it's a dream home that you desire, build it! If it's a degree that you want to obtain, enroll in somebody's college or university! If it is a dream career that you seek, get it! Whatever your "IT" is, make it happen! Chase it down, leap on top of it, and don't let it go until it comes to fruition.

Long gone are the days of I could have, should have, or would have. No more I'm too old, I'm not smart enough, or I can't do it like they can!

Today, I just came to ring the alarm for the dreamer inside of you! Get up! God has already promised that He would restore us back to the place in which we can dream again! He promised that everything we thought was desolate and obsolete in us, He would reawaken! So as we move forward, I encourage you to write down your dreams. Make a plan on what and how you can accomplish them. Push past every distraction that will attempt to defer you from your dream. Surround yourself with people who will support your dream! And last but not least, MAKE IT HAPPEN!

Reflection Questions

1. Have you ever been in a place where you no longer dreamed?
2. What happened in your life that caused you to end up in that place?
3. What dreams did you have that have subtly slipped away?
4. What strategies can you put in place to recapture and make those dreams come to fruition?

Day 2

THE WILLOW TREE PARABLE

One of the most intricate characteristics of a willow tree is its roots. The roots of a willow tree are known for its toughness, size, and its tenacity to life. The willow tree is a relatively small tree without much of a trunk. Its branches are long and bending, however, they give the appearance of being weak and fragile. Yet when a storm rages, it is the willow tree that stands strong.

Under the earth, the roots of the willow tree run long and wide. These roots hold the willow tree in place during the attacks from the violent winds. The deceptive branches are also strength for the willow tree. Even without a large trunk the willow tree branches are long and pliable. During a raging storm, the branches move and stretch with the wind, ever bending, but never breaking.

A valuable trait of the willow is its flexibility. The willow is one of the few trees that can bend in outrageous positions without snapping. This is a powerful metaphor for those of us on a spiritual path or search for endurance. The message here is to adjust with life rather than fighting it. To further the testimony to its adaptability, it is the willow's ability to not only survive, but to thrive in some of the most challenging conditions. Is this your testimony?

Reflect for just a moment. How many times have the tumultuous storms of life forced you to bend and stretch and be completely uncomfortable to the point where you felt as if you were going to break? But like the willow tree, your roots are strong. They run long into the ground. You are firmly planted, so even though life will make you feel like you are about to break, the only thing that is occurring is that your true strength and power to endure are coming to the forefront. So instead of trying to fight the storms of life, embrace them. Bend and move with them. Show life what tough roots, a little flexibility, and a lot of strength can and will do for you.

So let our prayer be, "Lord thank you for my sturdy roots that are planted in You. Help me to continue to bend with the storms of life, but never to break. I am strong because You are strong. I am unbreakable because You are unbreakable. I am a willow tree."

Reflection Questions

1. Describe a time in your life in which you felt that you were at your breaking point.
2. How did you overcome that situation/issue?
3. What kept you from completely letting go?

Day 3

First Comes Humility, then Comes Honor

Proverbs 16:18
> Pride goeth before destruction, and an haughty spirit before a fall.

In case you haven't realized it, God has called each one of us to be leaders and examples for others to follow that lead to Him. We are all highly gifted and talented, however, in order for us to operate effectively in our gifts and talents, we must do so with a spirit of humility. Humility is to be marked by meekness or modesty in behavior, attitude, or spirit. Simply put, humility is the opposite of arrogance.

Proverbs 16:18 in The Message Bible reads like this:

"First pride, then the crash—the bigger the ego, the harder the fall." In this scripture, the author gives us a very clear inclination of what will happen to us if we are prideful and egotistical with our God-given gifts, talents, and anointing if we do not operate with a spirit of humility. If you are prideful or arrogant, there will be a crash. If you have a big ego and you do things to be seen or noticed or praised by people, expect a hard fall. Only the things that you do with humility for Christ's sake will last.

Now this doesn't mean that you shouldn't be confident in yourself or what God had placed inside of you. Romans 12:3 says, *"For I say, through the grace given unto me, to every man that is among you, NOT TO THINK OF HIMSELF MORE HIGHLY THAN HE OUGHT TO THINK; but to think soberly, according as God hath dealt to every man the measure of faith"* (emphasis added). Just make sure that you are always utilizing your gift mix in such a way that God, not you, is being glorified.

So let our prayer be, "God thank you for the gifts and talents that you have blessed me with. Help me to remain humble while operating in them so that you will always get the glory. Amen."

Reflection Questions

1. In your own words, what do you think it means to "think more highly of yourself?"
2. What can you do to assure that you are not operating with a spirit of haughtiness?

Day 4

OBEDIENCE IS ALWAYS BETTER THAN SACRIFICE

I Samuel 15:22-23 (NLT)
> But Samuel replied, "What is more pleasing to the Lord: your burnt offerings and sacrifices or your obedience to His voice? Listen! Obedience is better than sacrifice, and submission is better than offering the fat of rams. Rebellion is as sinful as witchcraft, and stubbornness as bad as worshiping idols. So because you have rejected the command of the Lord, He has rejected you as king."

In this chapter of First Samuel, the Lord is rejecting Saul as the king of Israel. The Lord gave Saul concise instructions through Samuel. His instruction was to destroy ALL of the Amalekites and everything that belonged to them. As the story continues, Saul was sort of obedient, but not really. What this means is that he partially obeyed God. Yes, he killed MOST of the Amalekites and yes he destroyed MOST of their wealth and livestock, however, he captured and imprisoned the Amalekite king, Agag, and he kept what he thought was the best of the livestock.

For some reason we occasionally think that we know better than God. This is the only feasible explanation for us to hear God, receive clear instructions, and still not follow them. As Saul soon learned in the scripture, partial obedience is still disobedience. Saul's justification was that he saved the sheep and cattle to sacrifice back to God, but that's not what God told him to do. Our sacrifices mean nothing to God if our hearts aren't fully committed to following His instructions. We must understand that if God is requiring us to do something or give up something, He has something so much better waiting for us. We prolong and delay His blessings when we act in rebellion to His will. It is God's desire for us to be readily and willingly obedient to His voice, no hesitations, no compromising, just sheer obedience. It is only then when we can live in His complete fullness.

So as we move forward, let us be mindful of subtle rebellion that attempts to rise up in us and cause us to do contrary to what it is that God is requiring of us. Let our prayer be, "Lord I wholeheartedly submit to Your will and Your way. I want to be obedient to You in every area of my life. As I am obedient, I pray that my sacrifices will be acceptable in Your sight."

Reflection Questions

1. Take a minute to think. What areas in your life have you been subtly disobedient to God, whether knowingly or unknowingly?
2. Identify 2-3 ways that you can be more obedient to Him.

Day 5

MOVING FORWARD IS TOO RISKY; BUT GOING BACK IS TOO COSTLY

Exodus 14:10-14 (NLT)
> As Pharaoh approached, the people of Israel looked up and panicked when they saw the Egyptians overtaking them. They cried out to the Lord, and they said to Moses, "Why did you bring us out here to die in the wilderness? Weren't there enough graves for us in Egypt? What have you done to us? Why did you make us leave Egypt? Didn't we tell you this would happen while we were still in Egypt? We said, 'Leave us alone! Let us be slaves to the Egyptians. It's better to be a slave in Egypt than a corpse in the wilderness!'" But Moses told the people, "Don't be afraid. Just stand still and watch the Lord rescue you today. The Egyptians you see today will never be seen again. The Lord himself will fight for you. Just stay calm."

Most of us are familiar with the story told in Exodus 14. God gave Moses precise instruction on leading the Israelites out of Egypt. As the Israelites marched from Egypt, the Pharaoh sent his army to capture the Israelites and bring them back. So as the Egyptian soldiers neared the Israelites, conversations were initiated between the Israelites and Moses.

The Israelites began to bring charges against Moses. They began to ask, "Why did you bring us out here to die? Why didn't you leave us in Egypt?" They even told Moses that they would rather be slaves in Egypt than to be corpses in the wilderness! Essentially, what the Israelites were saying is that they would rather go back to bondage and live a substandard life that is not the one God intended for them to live, but instead is comfortable and familiar. Taking the risk of moving forward into a place of unfamiliarity would require them to relinquish all faith in themselves and put it all into God's all-knowing Hands.

Can you relate? Are you standing at the cusp of your destiny, staring it in the face? Are your knees trembling and stomach churning because you don't know what lies ahead? And although you know whatever you are moving forward into is risky and you are definitely taking a chance, you also realize that it is too costly to go backwards to the place of bondage that God has already delivered you from. Even though that place is comfortable, even though that place is familiar, you can't afford to back track. You can't afford old habits. You can't afford old ways of thinking. You can't afford old relationships that took more than they gave. You can't afford it! Going back will cost you too much peace, too much joy, too much sanity, too many tears, too much time, and ultimately, too much of your destiny!

So today I encourage you to take heed to the words Moses spoke in verse 13. *"Don't be afraid. Just stand still and watch the Lord rescue you today."* Take the leap of faith that God is requiring of you to go forward into the place that He has already prepared for you. Don't look back! When your past calls, don't answer! It has nothing new to say!

Reflection Questions

1. What will moving backwards cost you?
2. What risks will you be taking in moving forward?
3. Which is greater?

Day 6

CHANGE YOUR MIND

Mark 2:21-22 (NLT)
> "Besides, who would patch old clothing with new cloth? For the new patch would shrink and rip away from the old cloth, leaving an even bigger tear than before. "And no one puts new wine into old wineskins. For the wine would burst the wineskins, and the wine and the skins would both be lost. New wine calls for new wineskins."

This year has been a world wind year for me and for so many that are close to me as well. Our seasons have changed quickly and drastically. Now this change has mainly been good, so there are no complaints. However, one thing that I've noticed is that no matter how our situations and lives have changed, if we don't change our minds concerning certain aspects, we will remain the same.

We can't live in newness with the same old mind set. We can't know what we've known, see what we've seen, or hear what we've heard and continue to operate in the same manner in which we have been doing. The scripture tells us that we can't put old wine into new wineskins. If you do, the wineskin will burst and the wine will be wasted. We don't have another moment to waste any more opportunities. Old wine and new wine skins are not compatible with one another.

Now the same way that new wineskins are not capable of holding old wine, we are not able to think, act, speak, behave, and operate the way we have been doing. It won't work in the new place that God is calling us to. The Lord's desire is to elevate and increase, but He knows that if we have not changed our minds, we will mess up His plans. So as we move forward, ask and allow the Lord to change your mind. He wants us to see, do, be, and experience so much more, but we can only do so with a renewed mind. Let go of the old wineskins. New wine calls for new wineskins.

Reflection Questions

1. How can changing your perception or the way you think propel you in moving forward?
2. What would be some possible repercussions of you choosing not to let go of old ways of thinking?

Day 7

Extreme Makeover

Jeremiah 18:1-10 (The Message)
> GOD told Jeremiah, "Up on your feet! Go to the potter's house. When you get there, I'll tell you what I have to say." So I went to the potter's house, and sure enough, the potter was there, working away at his wheel. Whenever the pot the potter was working on turned out badly, as sometimes happens when you are working with clay, the potter would simply start over and use the same clay to make another pot. Then GOD's Message came to me: "Can't I do just as this potter does, people of Israel?" GOD's Decree! "Watch this potter. In the same way that this potter works his clay, I work on you, people of Israel. At any moment I may decide to pull up a people or a country by the roots and get rid of them. But if they repent of their wicked lives, I will think twice and start over with them. At another time I might decide to plant a people or country, but if they don't cooperate and won't listen to me, I will think again and give up on the plans I had for them.

In this passage God uses a potter to teach Jeremiah a lesson. The Lord sends Jeremiah down to the potter's house to help him gain understanding. God shows Jeremiah how the potter works diligently to create his masterpieces. He then allows Jeremiah to see the potter destroy his creation and start over when it doesn't turn out right.

So what could have possibly caused the potter to destroy what he has been so diligently working on? There may have been some blemishes in the clay. This is how our lives are. God diligently works on us. However, sins like disobedience, pride, ego, rebellion, being out of order, jealousy, envy, and greed cause us (the clay) to be messed up. However, God, who is the Potter, can take us in our most deformed shape and destroy all of those things in us and start over and ultimately make and mold us into who and what He wants us to be.

The Master Potter wants to shape our lives into a vessel for His glory, if we would only wholeheartedly submit our vessels to Him. So let our prayer be, "Lord thank You for constantly making and molding me into what You want me to be. Help me to be open to Your molding because I know that You are the Master Potter and You are making me into a masterpiece that can and will be used for Your glory."

Reflection Questions

1. What are some specific areas/issues in your life in which you need the Lord to destroy and remake you? Try to list at least 3.
2. What is holding you back from completely allowing Him to do so?

Day 8

THE BLESSEDNESS IN BROKENNESS

Matthew 14:14-21

> And Jesus went forth, and saw a great multitude, and was moved with compassion toward them, and He healed their sick. And when it was evening, His disciples came to Him saying, This is a desert place, and the time is now past; send the multitude away, that they may go into the villages, and buy themselves victuals. But Jesus said unto them, They need not depart; give ye them to eat. And they say unto Him, We have here but five loaves, and two fishes. He said, Bring them hither to me. And He commanded the multitude to sit down on the grass, and took the five loaves, and the two fishes, and looking up to heaven, He blessed, and brake, and gave the loaves to His disciples, and the disciples to the multitude. And they did all eat, and were filled: and they took up the fragments that remained twelve baskets full. And they that had eaten were about five thousand men, besides women and children.

In this scripture a dilemma has arisen. After a long day of miracle working among the multitudes of people, it is time for the crowd to eat, but there are only two fish and five loaves of bread with a crowd of more than five thousand people. The disciples suggested sending the people home to eat, but Jesus commanded that they feed the people. Now to the human mind, feeding five thousand people with two fish and five loaves of bread is inconceivable, but we know that with God all things are possible. As the scripture continues, Jesus took the two fish and five loaves of bread, blessed it, broke it, and was able to feed all of the people to the point where they were full and there was even a surplus of food left over. How was Jesus able to do such a thing? After He blessed it, He then broke it, and as He continued to break it, the food continued to multiply.

So how does this same principle work for us? Often times God wants to release His promised blessings to us, but we refuse to allow Him to break us. In the scripture, even though Jesus had blessed the bread and the fish, it wasn't until He broke it that the blessing was released and the multitudes were fed. By refusing and shying away from the breaking process, we tie the Hand of God that keeps attempting and desiring to bless us.

In our current state of unbrokenness, if the Lord released some of the things that He promised, we would mishandle, misuse, and even abuse His blessings. Therefore we must allow the Lord to break us. We must allow God to chisel those things off of us that prevents Him from doing what He needs to do in and through us. So in order for us to walk into the abundant life that God has laid aside for us, we have to stop resisting the breaking process. God can't bless what He can't break. If we continue to refuse to be broken, we are refusing to be blessed.

As we move forward let our prayer be, "God thank you for the breaking. I know that even though the breaking is uncomfortable and far from easy, it is necessary. God help me to be open and accepting to it because I know that there is a blessing on the other side of this breaking."

Reflection Questions

1. Identify an area(s) in your life that you have struggled with allowing the Lord to break you in.
2. Why have you resisted the breaking process?
3. What rewards do you think will come forth if you really allow God to do His perfect work in you?

Day 9

I'VE GOT YOUR BACK!

Matthew 6:25-32
> Therefore I say unto you, Take no thought for your life, what ye shall eat, or what ye shall drink; nor yet for your body, what ye shall put on. Is not the life more than meat, and the body than raiment? Behold the fowls of the air: for they sow not, neither do they reap, nor gather into barns; yet your heavenly Father feedeth them. Are ye not much better than they? Which of you by taking thought can add one cubit unto his stature? And why take ye thought for raiment? Consider the lilies of the field, how they grow; they toil not, neither do they spin: And yet I say unto you, That even Solomon in all his glory was not arrayed like one of these. Wherefore, if God so clothe the grass of the field, which today is, and tomorrow is cast into the oven, shall he not much more clothe you, O ye of little faith? Therefore take no thought, saying, What shall we eat? or, What shall we drink? or, Wherewithal shall we be clothed? (For after all these things do the Gentiles seek) for your heavenly Father knoweth that ye have need of all these things.

If someone tells you, "I've got your back," what does that really mean? Usually when someone makes a statement like that, they are telling you that if you need something, they have no problem looking out for or helping you. So how does God prove to us that He really "has our back?" Many times we get so caught up in the "little things" of this world. We begin to worry or become anxious about how all of our needs will be met. When our money is low and our bills are high, we begin to worry about how this or that is going to get paid. Or when we are hungry and there is no food in the refrigerator we worry about how we are going to eat. We even get nervous when our clothes get old and worn and we know there is no money to purchase new garments.

But through all of these worries, we seemingly forget that God has already ensured us that He has our back! In the scripture, Jesus tells us to look at the birds in the air as an example. Birds don't work like humans. They don't have any type of job description and they are careless in the sight of God, however He takes care of them, making sure that they never go lacking. So if God takes care of birds that don't do anything to build or enhance His kingdom, don't you think that He will surely take care of you? Someone who diligently works and seeks Him?

Jesus then goes on to talk about the flowers in the field. He talks about how beautiful they are. If God would give so much attention to flowers that most people will never have the opportunity to see, don't you think He will take pride in and do His very best for you, His wonderful workmanship? If God will look out for, make ways out of no way, make provision, create opportunities, and supply the needs for birds and flowers, how much more will He take care of you?

As we go forward, let us go with even more confidence and assurance that God has our back. He is already making things work on your behalf. Even if you can't see, trust Him. Stay focused on Christ and watch Him take care of you!

Reflection Questions

1. Do you genuinely believe that God is your source and that He alone provides all of our resources?
2. If yes to the first question, what is there to be anxious, worried, or even fearful about?

Day 10

ALL FAITH NO FEAR

II Timothy 1:7
> For God hath not given us the spirit of fear; but of power, and of love, and of a sound mind.

In this scripture, the Apostle Paul is telling Timothy that fear is not one of the gifts that God gives us. Understand that fear is not real. It is a crippling illusion from the devil that is used to hold our destiny and our purpose hostage. Fear is destructive! We must understand that it is one of the many things that God has already given us authority to defeat.

In place of fear, God gives us
1. Power – this is boldness, strength, and courage.
2. Love – this is compassion and understanding.
3. Sound Mind – this is peace and sanity.

Paul hints in this passage that Timothy had a timid personality by nature. You may not consider yourself to be a bold or courageous person but neither did Timothy. Yet God still used Timothy in a mighty way. He used him to stand side by side with Paul and preach and teach and even lead early Christians.

It is when we freely allow ourselves to operate in God's power, love, and peace that He can use our lives in such a mighty way that will bring Him glory. It is not how you feel about yourself that matters. It's not even about your natural personality or your personal profile. What matters most is the power of God in your life. He will use you beyond what you could ever expect or imagine. The only thing you have to do is let go of your fears and fully embrace the power, the love, and the sound mind that Christ offers.

So let our prayer be, "Lord, thank You for giving me courage to conquer every fear that has held me back from fully pursuing the things of You. I choose to no longer allow fear to hold me hostage or keep me in bondage. I choose to operate with a spirit of boldness through You."

Reflection Questions

1. What deceptive fears has the enemy tricked you into believing that have held you back from being and doing what God has called you to be and do?
2. What thoughts and feelings did you have that caused you to believe the enemy's lies?
3. What will you do from this moment forward to keep those fears at bay so that they no longer have power over you?

Day 11

GO GET 'EM SOLDIER

Ephesians 6:10-17
> Finally, my brethren, be strong in the Lord, and in the power of his might. Put on the whole armour of God, that ye may be able to stand against the wiles of the devil. For we wrestle not against flesh and blood, but against principalities, against powers, against the rulers of the darkness of this world, against spiritual wickedness in high places. Wherefore take unto you the whole armour of God, that ye may be able to withstand in the evil day, and having done all, to stand. Stand therefore, having your loins girt about with truth, and having on the breastplate of righteousness; And your feet shod with the preparation of the gospel of peace; Above all, taking the shield of faith, wherewith ye shall be able to quench all the fiery darts of the wicked. And take the helmet of salvation, and the sword of the Spirit, which is the word of God.

One of the devil's tactics or strategies is to attempt to "wear us out." He uses people, jobs, finances, our emotions, circumstances, and anything else that he can get his filthy little hands on to try to spiritually drain us to the point where we no longer even feel like fighting. But I love how Paul encourages us in this scripture to *"be strong in the Lord and the power of HIS might"* (emphasis added). He then tells us to put on God's whole armor, which means instead of trying to fight these spiritual battles with carnal weapons, gird up in your spiritual war clothes and prepare for the war ahead!

The devil isn't playing, so why are we? The enemy is trying to produce weary and faint saints, but that is not the will of the Father. So I double dog dare you to gird your loins with TRUTH. Go ahead and cover your heart with RIGHTEOUSNESS. Lace your feet with the gospel of PEACE. Now don't forget your shield of FAITH. That's going to protect you! Definitely put on your hat of SALVATION. But most importantly, make sure you never leave home without your sword which is the WORD that is embedded inside of you.

You are looking like you are ready to fight! Go get 'em soldier! You are looking mighty God STRONG! No weary saints over here. The devil better watch out because this soldier is ready for war!

Reflection Questions

1. Has the enemy tried to spiritually "wear you down?" If yes, explain how.
2. What are plans you can put into place to not only fight back, but to be victorious? List at least 2 strategies.

Day 12

FROM FECES TO FERTILIZER

Romans 8:28
> And we know that all things work together for good to them that love God, to them who are the called according to his purpose.

Feces are defined as waste matter eliminated from the animals' bowels and is also known as excrement. Fertilizer is any organic or inorganic material of natural or synthetic origin that is added to soil to supply one or more plant nutrients essential to the growth of plants. Fertilizer is often made from animal manure, such as cow and horse manure. What occurs is the natural chemicals from the manure burns off all of the bad elements from the roots of the plant which then enhances the growth process of the plant. So something that people view as disgusting, dirty, nasty, and waste can then be turned around and used to make plants (fruits and vegetables) that are essential to our well-being.

Now if God can take feces and turn it into fertilizer which is used to make things grow, surely He can take every failure, heartbreak, heartache, disappointment, setback, sorrow, dry place, loss, and delay, and turn it into something that will cause you or even someone else to grow!

Instead of focusing on all of the bad things that have happened in your life, change your perspective. Think about how those negative things caused you to evolve into the God strong person that you are today. All of those past setbacks were things that God knew He could use to burn off the waste in you and cultivate you so that the best part of you can come forth. Remember, God doesn't waste pain. God doesn't waste disappointment. God doesn't waste tribulation. God doesn't waste heartbreak. He has a plan for all of those things and in some way or another He will use those things to help you grow.

So let our prayer be, "God thank You for everything that has occurred in my life up until this point, even the things that I thought were working against me. God thank You for using those situations to make me into exactly who You've called me to be. Thank You for turning the waste in me into fertilizer that has only helped me to grow."

Reflection Questions

1. Recall a moment in your life that you considered to be a failure or a setback. Describe that moment.
2. How did that moment help develop you into the person you are today?

Day 13

LOVE WITHOUT LIMITS

Romans 8:35-39
> Who shall separate us from the love of Christ? Shall tribulation, or distress, or persecution, or famine, or nakedness, or peril, or sword? As it is written, for thy sake we are killed all the day long; we are accounted as sheep for the slaughter. Nay, in all these things we are more than conquerors through him that loved us. For I am persuaded, that neither death, nor life, nor angels, nor principalities, nor powers, nor things present, nor things to come, Nor height, nor depth, nor any other creature, shall be able to separate us from the love of God, which is in Christ Jesus our Lord.

Unconditional love is known as affection without limitations. It is the type of love that has no boundaries and is unchanging. In Romans 8:35-39, Paul discusses Christ's unconditional love for us. He boldly asks the question, *"What can separate us from the love of Christ?"* He then lists a few things that we could possibly think that could separate us from Christ's love. These things include:

1. Tribulation – troubles
2. Distress – anxiety or worrying
3. Persecution – mistreatment by others
4. Famine/Nakedness – lack
5. Peril/Sword – danger

These are all things that we deal with as we go through life, but none of these things or our response to them can ever cause God to stop loving us. In verse 38, Paul lets us know that he is persuaded or totally convinced that nothing in all the earth, including ourselves and our actions can make God not love us. Even when we do things that make God angry or that grieve Him, His unconditional, limitless love causes Him to offer us new mercies and sufficient grace. This is so because He still loves us and wants the absolute best for us. He is always there waiting on us with open arms like the loving Father that He is.

So let our prayer be, "God thank You for Your unconditional love that You freely offer to me. Help me to understand and take hold to Your love and offer it freely to others."

Reflection Questions

1. Are there issues or situations in your life that are preventing you from totally embracing the authentic love that Christ has for you?
2. What are some things that you could do to share the same unconditional love that Christ shows you to others?

Day 14

CHECK YOUR MOTIVES

> Matthew 7:22-23 (The Message)
> "Knowing the correct password—saying 'Master, Master,' for instance—isn't going to get you anywhere with me. What is required is serious obedience—doing what my Father wills. I can see it now—at the Final Judgment thousands strutting up to me and saying, 'Master, we preached the Message, we bashed the demons, our God-sponsored projects had everyone talking.' And do you know what I am going to say? 'You missed the boat. All you did was use me to make yourselves important. You don't impress me one bit. You're out of here.'

A motive is your reason or purpose for doing something. When you do something for somebody, why do you do it? For example, when you see someone struggling and you stop to lend a helping hand, why are you helping them out? Or when you use your gifts and talents like singing or dancing, why are you doing it?

Are you lending a helping hand because you know that God has blessed you to be a blessing or are you doing it to go back and brag to others about how you helped someone? When you use your gift mix, are you doing so to bring glory to God and so that others can see Christ's work in you, or are you doing it to put on a show so that people can congratulate and tell you how great and grand you are? Please know that Christ is not pleased with the works that we do for our names' sake. He is not impressed when we use what He has blessed us with to bring vain glory to ourselves, or in other words to make ourselves look good. Everything that we do in our lives should be done to show the world how amazing and magnificent is our God. When people look at the works we do, they should not see some flesh-wrapped performance; they should see Christ working through us. Remember, only what you do for Christ will last!

So as we go forward remember to check your motives. Make sure that everything you do is done to the glory of God. Ask yourself before you do anything, "Am I doing this to show off, or am I doing this to make my God look good?"

Reflection Questions

1. Do you do right simply because it's right to do, or are you expecting some form of reward or recognition?
2. Are your reasons for doing good because you want to bring glory to God or yourself?

Day 15

THERE IS NO NEED FOR COMPETITION IN THE BODY OF CHRIST

Luke 22:24-30 (The Message)
> Within minutes they were bickering over who of them would end up the greatest. But Jesus intervened: "Kings like to throw their weight around and people in authority like to give themselves fancy titles. It's not going to be that way with you. Let the senior among you become like the junior; let the leader act the part of the servant. "Who would you rather be: the one who eats the dinner or the one who serves the dinner? You'd rather eat and be served, right? But I've taken my place among you as the one who serves. And you've stuck with me through thick and thin. Now I confer on you the royal authority my Father conferred on me so you can eat and drink at my table in my kingdom and be strengthened as you take up responsibilities among the congregations of God's people.

In this passage of scripture, Jesus is having the Last Supper with His disciples. During the Supper the disciples began to argue over who would be the greatest disciple after Jesus was gone, as if discipleship was a competition. Jesus then stops them from arguing to teach them a lesson. His message was simple; none of them were greater than the other. There was no need to be competitive in doing the work of Christ. He then tells them to take up the responsibilities of the congregation. This means GO DO THE WORK!

So how does this relate to us as 21st century Christians? There is no need for competition in the body of Christ. There is enough work to be done in the Kingdom of God for everybody to have their own individual tailor made assignment. No need to lust after or covet someone else's assignment. We must support and encourage one another's gifting and talents because God has given every one of us our own unique anointing and a sufficient amount of grace to complete our assignment. So today ask the Lord, "What is it that I have been assigned to do and how can I complete your work?" Then seek Him for guidance on how to accomplish it.

Reflection Questions

1. What is your assignment?
2. Now that you've identified your assignment, what is your plan to complete or finish the task at hand?

Day 16

NO COMPROMISING

Luke 4:5-8
> And the devil, taking him up into an high mountain, shewed unto him all the kingdoms of the world in a moment of time. And the devil said unto him, All this power will I give thee, and the glory of them: for that is delivered unto me; and to whomsoever I will I give it. If thou therefore wilt worship me, all shall be thine. And Jesus answered and said unto him, Get thee behind me, Satan: for it is written, Thou shalt worship the Lord thy God, and him only shalt thou serve.

To compromise means *to arrive at a settlement by making concessions, or to reduce the quality, value, or degree of something.* In the scripture as Jesus is in the wilderness, He has an encounter with satan. As the scripture continues, satan tries to tempt Jesus, or simply put, he tried to get Jesus to compromise. It was satan's desire to decrease the value of Jesus' purpose and assignment while in the wilderness.

How many times does satan try this same trick with you? How often does the enemy slither his way into your thoughts and try to show you how good things could be if you would only compromise your faith? Compromise your obedience? Compromise your anointing? Compromise your destiny? How frequent does he try to get you to say or do things that are contrary to what God has told you?

Now when you have these encounters, how do you respond? Do you fall for the enemy's tired compromising tactics, or do you take on the stature Jesus had in the wilderness and boldly put satan in his place, which is behind you? God is calling you to be an uncompromising servant that is determined to do the work of the Kingdom His way. He is not searching for hearts that want to take the shortcut to His glory. He is looking for you to be a person that is willing to be steadfast, unmovable, and always abounding in Him. So let our prayer be, "Lord help me to be strong and uncompromising in You. Even though I know the enemy is going to try to convince me to live contrary to Your will, I know that Your will and Your way is the best way for me."

Reflection Questions

1. How has the enemy attempted to get you to compromise on what God has told you?
2. How do you respond when he tries to get you to compromise?

Day 17

I AM WHAT YOU SEE

Psalm 139:14-18
> I will praise thee; for I am fearfully and wonderfully made: marvellous are thy works; and that my soul knoweth right well. My substance was not hid from thee, when I was made in secret, and curiously wrought in the lowest parts of the earth. Thine eyes did see my substance, yet being unperfect; and in thy book all my members were written, which in continuance were fashioned, when as yet there was none of them. How precious also are thy thoughts unto me, O God! how great is the sum of them! If I should count them, they are more in number than the sand: when I awake, I am still with thee.

A few years ago, I was dealing with an issue. During that time, a friend of mine called and began to minister to my spirit. She led me to understand that the reason I was allowing some of the circumstances that were occurring in my life to continue was because I did not see myself the way God saw me. She led me to Psalm 139. Sometimes we forget, or are even oblivious to the fact that we are God's perfect creation. This doesn't mean that we are perfect creatures, but what it does mean is that when God created us, He took His time. He put so much thought and effort into you to make and mold you into a beautiful masterpiece, not missing anything. This is why the writer is in awe of God's creation.

When we come to the conclusion that God's perception of us is the only one that matters, we will refuse to settle for anything less than God's best for us and our lives. We won't put up with certain people, feelings, ungodly habits, or any other trash that attempts to reside in our lives. We must grasp hold to the fact that God's thoughts of us are so grand, even in our many imperfections and mess ups. He still takes pride in us. Through setbacks and mistakes, His opinion about us never changes. If we are good enough for God, we are good enough for ourselves.

So as we move ahead, let our prayer be, "Lord, help me to see me in the same manner in which You see me. Thank You for not allowing my imperfections to change Your thoughts toward me. As I began to see myself through Your eyes, help me not to settle or allow anything in my life that would take away from the value of Your creation."

Reflection Questions

1. What lies has the enemy attempted to make you believe concerning who and what you are?
2. List 5 things that are absolutely amazing about you.
3. How do those things contradict what the enemy has said to and about you?

Day 18

CRUCIFYING THE SPIRIT OF THE WASTER

Proverbs 18:9
> He also that is slothful in his work is brother to him that is a great waster.

For entirely too long, one of my major struggles has been time. Sometimes it seems like no matter how hard I try being on time anywhere is difficult. Even when I get up earlier, prepare myself in advance, and plan, I still end up being late. This became such an issue that I went to my pastor for insight and advice. It was then that she told me that I had to deal with the root of the problem. As hard of a pill as it was to swallow, I had to deal with the fact that I was battling the spirit of a waster. I never thought of myself as someone who wasted anything, but that was my reality.

According to dictionary.com, the word waste, in the context of a verb, means t*o be consumed, spent, or employed uselessly or without giving full value or being fully utilized or appreciated.* When it came to time, I consumed it uselessly. I didn't value it. I couldn't properly utilize it. And I definitely didn't appreciate it. These are all characteristics of the spirit of a waster.

The spirit of a waster is inconsiderate. It is selfish. It is disrespectful. It is lazy. It is slothful. It is ungrateful. It is careless. It has no discipline. It doesn't operate in obedience

It is often reckless. It is tactless. It is rebellious. It is a thief. And it has no boundaries.

The spirit of a waster always has procrastination riding on its back. This spirit will cause you to negate responsibilities, miss opportunities, squander over blessings, withhold God ordained impartation from others, and – if it lurks too long – completely miss your destiny. Can you afford that? Are you willing to allow this spirit to rob you anymore than it already has? If the answer to these questions are no, then it's time to take action.

So today we come against the spirit of the waster. We crucify it at its root. No longer will it steal, kill, or destroy our dreams, our goals, or our destiny. For too long it has tricked and deceived us, but no more! We speak death to its assignment to destroy our lives. We will be disciplined. We will be obedient. And we reclaim everything that the spirit of the waster has taken from us. In Jesus' name!

Reflection Questions

1. Has the spirit of the waster showed up in any parts of your life? If so, explain.
2. What effect has this spirit had on your life? What have you missed out on because of it?
3. What plan can you put into action to effectively combat and kill this spirit?

Day 19
WHAT ARE YOU DOING WITH YOUR TALENTS?

Matthew 25: 14-28 (NLT)
> "Again, the Kingdom of Heaven can be illustrated by the story of a man going on a long trip. He called together his servants and entrusted his money to them while he was gone. He gave five bags of silver to one, two bags of silver to another, and one bag of silver to the last— dividing it in proportion to their abilities. He then left on his trip. "The servant who received the five bags of silver began to invest the money and earned five more. The servant with two bags of silver also went to work and earned two more. But the servant who received the one bag of silver dug a hole in the ground and hid the master's money. "After a long time their master returned from his trip and called them to give an account of how they had used his money. The servant to whom he had entrusted the five bags of silver came forward with five more and said, 'Master, you gave me five bags of silver to invest, and I have earned five more.' "The master was full of praise. 'Well done, my good and faithful servant. You have been faithful in handling this small amount, so now I will give you many more responsibilities. Let's celebrate together! "The servant who had received the two bags of silver came forward and said, 'Master, you gave me two bags of silver to invest, and I have earned

> two more.' "The master said, 'Well done, my good and faithful servant. You have been faithful in handling this small amount, so now I will give you many more responsibilities. Let's celebrate together!' "Then the servant with the one bag of silver came and said, 'Master, I knew you were a harsh man, harvesting crops you didn't plant and gathering crops you didn't cultivate. I was afraid I would lose your money, so I hid it in the earth. Look, here is your money back.' "But the master replied, 'You wicked and lazy servant! If you knew I harvested crops I didn't plant and gathered crops I didn't cultivate, why didn't you deposit my money in the bank? At least I could have gotten some interest on it.' "Then he ordered, 'Take the money from this servant, and give it to the one with the ten bags of silver.

Most of us are familiar with this story. In this biblical account, Jesus uses the parable of the master and his servants. The master gave each of his servants talents or investments. To one he gave five, to one he gave two, and to another he gave one.

The first two servants took their talents and went out and shared or invested them. The talents then doubled. The servant with only one talent was afraid (because he had so few) that instead of going out and trading his talent, he hid it in the ground. When the master came back he blessed the two servants that went out and used and doubled their talents, however, he cursed and took away the talents of the servant whom buried his in the ground.

So how does this lesson apply to us? The Lord has blessed us with many gifts and talents that He want us to use to build His Kingdom, but the question is what are we doing with what God has blessed us with? Are we like the first two servants? Can God trust us to go out and use our gifts and talents to help His people? Or are we like the third servant who was so afraid of possibly losing that we sit on our gifts, even though we know that there are people and a world who need what we have? God wants to entrust us with more, but if we can't properly handle what He has already given us, then He won't offer us more. When we use what He has given us, the Lord will bless it and multiply it. On the other hand, when we allow the enemy to trick us or scare us out of using what God has placed down inside of us the Lord will not only be displeased, but He will take it away.

So let our prayer be, "Lord thank You for the gifts that You have placed inside of me. Help me to not let anything prevent me from freely using those talents that I possess. God I offer them back to You to be used for Your glory."

Reflection Questions

1. What are you doing with the gifting and talents that God has blessed you with?
2. Can God trust you with more? Why or why not?

Day 20
What I Learned From a Sea Turtle

Galatians 9:6
> And let us not be weary in well doing: for in due season we shall reap, if we faint not.

When sea turtles are born or when they hatch, they do so on sand. Now even though the ocean is the sea turtle's natural habitat, only about 1 in 20 sea turtles actually make it into the ocean. This happens because every time the turtles get closer to the water, the ocean pushes them back. And this process continuously happens. The one turtle that reaches the ocean is the one who makes up in his mind, that regardless of the fact that they are going to get pushed back, they NEVER give up!

The sea turtle understands that the opposition of the ocean is going to come, but he is also aware that he has what it takes to make it to the ocean if he just keeps pressing forward. Galatians 9:6 says. "And let us not be weary in well doing: for in due season we shall reap, if we faint not." I believe that the one sea turtle who makes it into the ocean takes on this same mindset. The sea turtle knows that regardless of the pushback that the waves and the ocean will surely provide, he knows that it is his innate ability to make it into the ocean.

Simply put, the sea turtle understands that he is really built to last! The sea turtle realizes that the mechanism which grieves him the most – the ocean – is going to be the best thing for him.

So as we go forward, let us think and act like the sea turtle. Let us be reminded that we already have everything we need inside of us to be successful and sustained in the place where God has destined for us to be.

Reflection Questions

1. What "thing" can you think of that will cause you to hold on and keep pushing when life attempts to stop you from accomplishing what you know you have in you to do?
2. How can you use the opposition in your life to motivate you?

Day 21

First Things First: A Lesson in Prioritizing

Matthew 6:33
> But seek ye first the kingdom of God, and his righteousness; and all these things shall be added unto you.

In April of 2013, my car completely gave out on me as I drove home from work one afternoon. I had no money saved, my credit was shot, and I had no plan of what to do next. During the 7 day period wherein I was without my own personal vehicle, I had several obligations that I was committed to concerning my church. As much as I wanted to focus all of my attention on my own situation regarding my car, I knew that I could not negate the obligations I had to God and His house. Sooner than later, I was able to go to the car lot, pick out the vehicle that I wanted, and drive off the lot with no problem. But before I could do any of that, I had to prioritize.

To prioritize means *to determine the order for dealing with a series of items or tasks according to their relative importance.* In Matthew 6:33, Jesus gives us an excellent lesson on how to prioritize our lives. Frequently, prioritizing becomes difficult when "life" happens, and trials, tribulations, discomfort, and uncertainties are prevalent. It is not an easy task trying to keep your mind and focus on the works of Christ and His Kingdom when mayhem and chaos breaks out in your life. It becomes hard to give your full, undivided attention to the assignments that God has given you when your life seems to be upside down.

When situations like this occur, the act of prioritizing is a little more difficult. This is because you are looking at all of these other things occurring. These situations are attempting to rise up and make themselves appear bigger or greater than the business that God has entrusted you to handle.

One of the key concepts to effectively prioritizing is deciding which tasks are the most important; which task deserves your time, effort, and your energy? Learn to handle the big stuff first and I promise you, the things of God will always be the "big stuff." If we step back and look at our issues, our problems, our situations, and our business, they look tiny when perched beside our great big God! All we have to do is continue to fixate on the things of God and I assure you if you take care of His business, He will always take care of yours!

Reflection Questions

1. List your top 5 priorities.
2. Does your list include handling God's business first? If not, how can you reprioritize so that He is at the top?

Day 22

TO GET ABUNDANCE, MEDIOCRITY MUST DIE

John 10:10
> The thief cometh not, but for to steal, and to kill, and to destroy: I am come that they might have life, and that they might have it more abundantly.

Abundance is *an extremely plentiful or over-sufficient quantity or supply*. Some synonyms include: affluence, ampleness, fortune, opulence, plethora, prosperity, or thriving. The word mediocre means *of moderate quality or not very good*. Some synonyms include: ordinary, average, uninspired, undistinguished, indifferent, lack luster or forgettable.

I believe most of us have a clear understanding that there is a better life that God has designed and ordained for us to live than the one that we are living right now. So what is keeping us from living our best life now? One thing that we can clearly identify is mediocrity. Mediocrity is a tricky thing; it's tricky because it can be very subtle. Mediocrity is comfortable; it is lazy; it is stuck on tradition; it satisfies our flesh; it doesn't like to try new things or new ways of doing things; and it is complacent.

All of these things are contrary to what we know abundance to be. Abundance is hard working; it is uncomfortable; it is open to newness; it satisfies our spirit; and it is always searching for better and greater. So today, make a decision to stop allowing mediocrity to steal your dreams. Stop allowing mediocrity to kill your influence. Stop allowing mediocrity to destroy your purpose. Make a decision to curse and kill mediocrity at its root. Let's make a conscience choice to do something that we've never done in order to live the abundant life that God desires for us to live. Let mediocrity die!

Reflection Questions

1. What is keeping you from living your best life now?
2. In what ways can you identify how mediocrity has delayed or held you back from doing, being and receiving God's very best?

Day 23
KILL THE ROOT, KILL THE FRUIT

John 15:2-6 (NLT)
> He cuts off every branch of mine that doesn't produce fruit, and he prunes the branches that do bear fruit so they will produce even more. You have already been pruned and purified by the message I have given you. Remain in me, and I will remain in you. For a branch cannot produce fruit if it is severed from the vine, and you cannot be fruitful unless you remain in me. "Yes, I am the vine; you are the branches. Those who remain in me, and I in them, will produce much fruit. For apart from me you can nothing. Anyone who does not remain in me is thrown away like a useless branch and withers. <u>Such branches are gathered into a pile to be burned.</u>

Today we are here to lie to rest some things that have plagued us for entirely too long. We've tried for some time now to detach ourselves from these things, only to end up right back in the same place. We've prayed, we've fasted, we've quoted scripture, we've cried, and we've even pleaded for these things to be diminished in our lives, but they still seem to linger on and continue to resurface. We've petitioned, pulled down and casted out, but nothing seems to work. But today, we are going to put to death these crippling and seemingly immortal things!

So you say, "What are these THINGS that she keeps referring to?" I'm so glad you asked! These are the fruits that are continually being produced in our lives that refuse to die. Why won't they die? I'm glad you asked that too! They won't die because we've been attacking the fruit, but refusing to go after the root! What fruits have you been trying to kill that won't seem to die?

Some of us have tried to kill fear, anxiety, and even doubt, but they keep rearing their ugly heads. Today we put to death the root of lack of faith. That is the thing inside that causes us not to completely trust God without any hesitation or reservation.

Some of us have attempted to walk away from bitterness and resentment, but for some reason we can't evade them. Today we put to death the root of unforgiveness! We crucify those hurts and pains and broken places that we've refuse to allow to be healed for so long. We release them right now.

Some of us have consistently fought and lost the battle against disobedience. Today we put to death the root of rebellion. We execute the part of us that refuses to submit wholeheartedly to the authority and rule of God.

And as we exterminate these roots, we plant the roots of faith. We plant roots of love. We plant roots of agreement.

So let our prayer be, "God let my roots be in You. Let the fruit that I produce be pleasing to You. Lord kill every root in me that does not yield good fruit."

Reflection Questions

1. What reoccurring "fruits" have you been trying to kill that won't seem to die?
2. Take a moment to think. What "roots" are causing those same "fruits" not to die?

Day 24

REAL VERSUS FAKE: DEVELOPING AUTHENTIC FAITH

James 1:2-4 (The Message)
> Consider it a sheer gift, friends, when test and challenges come at you from all sides. You know that under pressure, your faith-life is forced into the open and shows its true colors. So don't try to get out of anything prematurely. Let it do its work so you become mature and well-developed, not deficient in any way.

When something is authentic that means it is bona fide, authoritative, genuine, verified, valid, and legitimate. If we all be honest, we've all had a "why me" moment. This is a moment in life in which we ask God, "Why am I the one going through this rough, unwarranted, underserved period in my life?"

The scripture above speaks directly to our "why me" moments. Trials and tribulations that we experience are never purposeless. They are hand picked lessons that God uses to authenticate our faith. There is a level of authenticity our faith must have before we can effectively convey it to others. Our faith gains authority when it is worked. If we are never put in situations where we have to work our faith, then it becomes a useless tool that can and never will accomplish anything.

The scripture urges us to not try to get out of tribulations prematurely. The challenges come to develop and mature us so that we aren't deficient or lacking in any way. Simply put, the stuff we go through are simple life lessons that God uses to give us opportunities to exercise and prove our faith to be strong. God is always looking for the chance to make Himself bigger in our lives. Challenges and hard times allot Him the chance to do so. God also uses these rough times to show us what we are really made of, and depending on our response to tribulations, it shows us areas in which we still need to be more developed. This is why we should look at these trials as gifts.

So let our prayer be, "Lord thank You for every hard time I've experienced in my life. I know that these are moments where You are strengthening and increasing my faith in You. Help me not to resist tribulation but to trust You even the more. Thank You for authenticating my faith."

Reflection Questions

1. Have you ever had a "WHY ME" moment? Describe that moment.
2. Once you made it through that rough moment, what did you learn from it?
3. What did you learn about your faith?

Day 25

I SHALL NOT BE MOVED

Acts 20:20-22
> And now, behold, I go bound in the spirit unto Jerusalem, not knowing the things that shall befall me there: Save that the Holy Ghost witnesseth in every city, saying that bonds and afflictions abide me. But none of these things move me, neither count I my life dear unto myself, so that I might finish my course with joy, and the ministry, which I have received of the Lord Jesus, to testify the gospel of the grace of God.

In this scripture, Paul was in a position where he was getting ready to embark on a transition in his life and in his ministry. And as uncertain as he was about this next phase of his life, he understood very clearly that it would not be an easy journey ahead. He knew that there would be hard times ahead. He knew that there would be those who doubted him. He knew that there would be those who falsely accused him. He knew that there would be some moments of feeling absolutely alone. He knew that he would even face imprisonment. However, even in his uncertainty, Paul knew that he had to move because the Holy Spirit was leading the way. Not transitioning was not an option!

Now how many of us are at or have been at this same crossroads in our own lives? We are transitioning into a new place that seems so much greater than anything we've ever experienced. We are stepping into territories that we never imagined our feet would touch. We are taking on an assignment that we feel we aren't qualified to complete. We are making some unpopular decisions. We are facing doubters and facing naysayers.

But let us take on the attitude that Apostle Paul had in the 24th verse. Let us take on that "but none of these things move me" attitude. Let us be reminded of how Paul understood that his next level really didn't have anything to do with him. And neither does ours! It always has been and it always will be about the cause of Christ! So expect attacks to come. Expect tribulation to pop up. Expect discomfort. Expect some alone moments. Expect criticism. But whatever you do, DON'T BE MOVED!

So let our prayer be, "Lord I understand that in this next season of my life there are going to be some difficulties and tough times ahead. But because I know that this is the path that You have laid aside for me, I will not be moved! God help me to stand firm in You and finish my course with joy!"

Reflection Questions

1. What reservations do you have concerning moving to your next level?
2. What can you do to firmly plant yourself so that you will not be moved by the opposition that you will possibly face?

Day 26

DON'T MISS YOUR EXIT

I Corinthians 10:13
> There hath no temptation taken you but such as is common to man: but God is faithful, who will not suffer you to be tempted above that ye are able; but will with the temptation also make a way to escape, that ye may be able to bear it.

Usually birds fly south in the winter. During the last snow storm that I experienced, I sat in my living room looking out the window as snow profusely fell from the sky. As I watched the snow cover the ground, I noticed a Red Robin attempting to fly and escape the snow. However, the harder the bird's wings flapped, the more difficult it became to fly. I began to ponder, why didn't this little birdie fly south with the other birdies? What caused this bird to get left behind? What caused him to miss his opportunity to avoid this crippling weather that he isn't genetically created to endure? How did he miss his chance to exit?

Was the birdie not in place when the flock flew south? Was he preoccupied? Did he not get the memo? There was already a plan in place that would have allowed the bird to elude the misfortune of the snowstorm; however, for some reason or another, the bird missed his exit!

Have you ever been the bird? Have you ever been in a situation where your back was up against a wall, pressure was all around you and all you wanted was a way out? Was there a time in life where you couldn't seem to find a way out? Remember that God is always there and He has already rendered a way out for you! Because He is so faithful, He has cleared the escape route! All you have to do is take it. Don't miss your exit!

So let our prayer be, "God thank you for not allowing any temptation to overtake me. Lord please give me insight to know and see the escape that you are providing."

Reflection Questions

1. Are there any situations in your life that you have been searching for a way out of?
2. Have you sought God to provide a way of escape?

Day 27

STAY FOCUSED

Philippians 4:8 (NLT)
> And now, dear brothers and sisters, one final thing. Fix your thoughts on what is true, and honorable, and right, and pure, and lovely, and admirable. Think about things that are excellent and worthy of praise.

To be distracted means to *cause to turn away from the original focus of attention or interest.* Another perception of distraction is to pull in conflicting emotional directions or to be unsettled. We all have been in a situation at one time or another in our lives in which we have been distracted, whether it was in school, on our jobs, or even in our homes. We had all intentions on completing an assignment, but somehow, someway, our attention was diverted from the task at hand.

Now as a result of being distracted, things were delayed and disorganized; our original plan was detoured; and sometimes the mission or task was not completed at all. The same way this occurs in our natural lives, it happens in our spiritual lives as well. God gives us an assignment and we work diligently at it for a while, but then here comes the enemy.

Understand that the enemy is smart enough to know that we are too committed to quit, so instead he begins to throw everything our way to distract us. He begins to attack your finances so now you are focused on financial obligations instead of the work of Christ. He begins to attack your family, so now you are focused solely on your spouse, children, or whoever else instead of the work of Christ. He begins to attack your health so you now are focused on getting well instead of the work of Christ.

Even though he hasn't gotten you to throw in the towel, he has created so many distractions that your attention has been shifted to everything except the assignment God has anointed, called, and ordained you to do. Remember, if the enemy can't get you to quit, he will try to have you absorbed with the issues of life.

So how are we going to maintain our spiritual focus? We are going to live out Philippians 4:8. By doing this, we leave no room for the enemy's distractions to take root and bear fruit in our lives. So let our prayer be, "Lord thank You for my assignment. God help me to stay focused on the things of You and only You. God, anything that attempts to distract me from Your word, I curse and kill it at its source. I thank You for Your mission in my life being completed."

Reflection Questions

1. Can you identify ways in which the enemy has attempted to distract you?
2. How did you respond to the distractions?
3. What are some things that you do to maintain your spiritual focus?

Day 28

SO WHAT ARE YOU SAYING??

Proverbs 29:11 (NLT)
> Fools vent their anger, but the wise quietly hold it back.

Proverbs 18:21 (The Message)
> Words kill, words give life; they're either poison or fruit—you choose.

Have you ever said something that hurt someone's feelings or that was out of place and as soon as it escaped your lips, you regretted it? We often times say the wrong things when we are angry. Because we are hurt, we say things that we know are down-right mean and vicious.

In the first scripture, the writer lets us know that in God's eyes, it is very foolish to say any and everything that comes to our minds. A fool does not take any consideration of his words before they come out of his mouth. He does not think about whether or not his words are hurtful, destructive, damaging, or just plain mean. He does not consider that once his words are spoken, they can never be taken back.

Now the second scripture vividly conveys to us the authority that our words have. Our words have the power to kill or give life to anything. It's our choice how we use them. As a representative of Christ, our words should never tear down, destroy, discourage, break someone's spirit, mislead, or kill. Instead, they should enlighten, improve, teach, build, encourage, motivate, push, call forth, and speak life!

So let our prayer be, "Lord help me to think before I speak. Let my words be pleasing to You. Let my words be life giving and not life taking, in Jesus' name. Amen.

Reflection Questions

1. Why do you think it is so vital to be mindful of the words that come from your mouth?
2. List at least 3 positive confessions over your life that you desire to see come to pass in your life.

Day 29

JUST A REMINDER

Psalm 23

In this scripture, David is simply reminding us of some things we already know, but may need a little refreshing.

He begins the Psalm by saying:

The Lord is my SHEPHERD: This represents relationship. This means that God promises to guard us, watch over us, and protect us.

I shall not want: This represents provision. This is a gentle reminder that God is our source and there is nothing that we need that His hand can't and won't provide.

He maketh me to lie down in green pastures: That's rest! This speaks to the peace that God offers us in the most troubling and trying times that we will ever experience.

He leadeth me beside the still waters: That's refreshment! This means that God allows us to be renewed when we need it.

He restoreth my soul: That's healing! This means that every broken or abused part of you, the Lord gives us the opportunity to experience wholeness in those areas.

He leadeth me in the paths of righteousness: That's guidance! This means that there is no need to attempt to map out our own lives, because the Lord will lead and direct every step that we take.

For his name's sake: That's purpose! This means that everything that we do should be done to glorify God.

Yea though I walk through the valley of the shadow of death: That's testing! This means that trials and tribulations will come; it's part of the territory.

I will fear no evil: That's protection! This means that even though the attacks will come, we are safe and secure in God.

For thou art with me: That's faithfulness! This is God's assurance to us that He is always watching out for us and is there to help in every situation.

Thou rod and thy staff they comfort me: That's discipline! This means that God loves us enough to chastise us ensuring that we don't abide in sin.

Thou preparest a table before me in the presence of mine enemies: That's hope! This means that even when wickedness and evil doers attempt to rise up against us, God will not only make their plans fail, but He will continue to bless us in the midst.

Thou anointest my head with oil: That's consecration! This means that God extends the opportunity to us to commit a life-long worship experience with Him.

My cup runneth over: That's abundance! This is God's promise of an abundant life, one in which He will give us more than we could ever think or desire.

Surely goodness and mercy shall follow me all the days of my life: That's blessings! This means that God will always be looking for opportunities to bless you!

And I will dwell in the house of the Lord: That's safety! There will always be security in the arms of God.

FOR EVER: That's eternity! These promises will follow us all the way through eternity!

This scripture provided us with many promises! So from this moment onward, let's continue to stand on the promises of God. Let's trust Him like never before to do what we know He is more than capable of doing!

Day 30

YOUR INFLUENCE

I Peter 2:9-12 (NLT)
> But you are not like that, for you are a chosen people. You are royal priests, a holy nation, God's very own possession. As a result, you can show others the goodness of God, for He called you out of the darkness into His wonderful light. "Once you had no identity as a people; now you are God's people. Once you received no mercy; now you have received God's mercy." Dear friends, I warn you as "temporary residents and foreigners" to keep away from worldly desires that wage war against your very souls. Be careful to live properly among your unbelieving neighbors. Then even if they accuse you of doing wrong, they will see your honorable behavior, and they will give honor to God when He judges the world.

Influence is *the capacity or power of persons or things to be a compelling force on or produce effects on actions, behavior, or opinions of others*. Each one of us has a stream of influence. Somebody somewhere is looking at our actions, our behavior, and listening to the words that come out of our mouths. And from that, they are making decisions for their own lives based off what they've seen and heard from us.

Our influence has the capability to go to places that our physical bodies will never have the opportunity to see.

This is why it is the enemy's desire to eradicate it. Our influence has a lasting impact on others because it has the chance to change their lives and the lives of all those who are connected to them. Our influence goes further than our minds can honestly conceive. The enemy knows this. This is why he wants us to say one thing and do another; teach one way and live another; preach righteousness and live corruptly. He wants the world to view believers as hypocrites and liars, and if we are representatives of Christ and this is how the world views us, how do you think they view our God?

This is why the scripture warns us to live "properly" amongst our unbelieving neighbors. The world won't turn to Christ by our words alone. Our actions and our lifestyles are the drum majors for our influence. This is why the scripture refers to us as a chosen people, God's very own possession. The Lord has set us aside so that He can use us and our lives as examples to show the world what He looks like. So let our prayer be, "Lord thank You for my influence. Let my thoughts, my words, and my actions reflect You in every way. Help me to always represent You properly. Let my influence always lead others to You."

Reflection Questions

1. If you were to ask someone that knows you, how would they describe your influence?
2. How does your lifestyle or your influence represent Christ?

Day 31

FROM RATCHETNESS TO RIGHTEOUSNESS

II Samuel 12:24
> And David comforted Bathsheba his wife, and went unto her, and lay with her: and she bare a son, and he called his name Solomon: and the Lord loved Him.

Most of us are familiar with the story of King David and Bathsheba that is told in Second Samuel, chapters 11 and 12. Bathsheba was Uriah's wife, one of David's faithful servants and a part of his army. While Uriah was away fighting, David saw Bathsheba bathing on the balcony and sent for her because he wanted to be with her. Everything about David's actions were ratchet. From not being in place on the battlefield, to lusting after Bathsheba, to abusing his power as king, to laying with Bathsheba, to being deceitful in trying to cover up Bathsheba's pregnancy, even down to him having Uriah murdered.

As the scriptures continue, we see David growing or becoming comfortable in his ratchet-*ness*. He is so at ease that after Uriah's death, he took Bathsheba in and made her his wife and planned to live life happily ever after as if nothing had ever happened. But God sent Nathan, the prophet, to get David to see for himself the ratchet-*ness* of his own actions. So how was it that David was able to move from this unscrupulous position he'd gotten himself into, to a place of righteousness?

The first thing David did once Nathan revealed his wrongdoing to him was to set right his relationship with God. He repented and asked for forgiveness. He didn't waddle in self-pity or condemnation; instead he took responsibility, got out of his feelings, and got back in right standing with God. When we get it right with God, that's when He can began to turn our ratchet-*ness* into righteousness. As wrong as the whole situation was concerning David and Bathsheba, once David made it right with God, God was able to bless them with Solomon, who was God's beloved. Solomon grew to be one of the wisest men ever to walk the face of this earth. He was a king like no other.

God can take your most ratchet moments or actions, forgive you, turn that ratchet into righteousness, and still get the glory. So let our prayer be, "God forgive me for my ratchet-*ness*. God restore me back to right standing with You. Use those things in my life that were meant to shame, embarrass, and keep me in bondage to show others Your true glory."

Reflection Questions

1. What shameful and unsavory moments in your life can you give to God so that He may use it for His glory?
2. Can you think of at least one person that would benefit from knowing the testimony of your ratchet-*ness*?

Day 32

JUST FORGET ABOUT IT

Micah 7:18-20 (NLT)
> Where is another God like you, who pardons the guilt of the remnant, overlooking the sins of His special people? You will not stay angry with your people forever, because you delight in showing unfailing love. Once again you will have compassion on us. You will trample our sins under your feet and throw them into the depths of the ocean! You will show us your faithfulness and unfailing love as you promised to our ancestors Abraham and Jacob long ago.

Have you ever wronged someone and then asked for forgiveness? And that person is compassionate and forgives you, but you have a hard time forgiving yourself? One of the hardest things to do is to forgive yourself when you've wronged someone. Occasionally I find this to be exceptionally true when it comes to my relationship with Christ. Because I reverence Him in the manner in which I do, it is hard to move forward after I have intentionally or unintentionally grieved Him. However, the scripture reminds us that when we repent, not only does He forgive us, but he throws our sins into the sea of forgetfulness. We can't even make God remember. His love for us keeps no record of our wrongs.

So why is it that God can forgive us, but we have such a hard time forgiving ourselves and moving on? It is the enemy's desire to hold you hostage to your past mistakes, slip ups, and bad decisions. He desires nothing more than for you to get stuck in a place of regret and never move forward in Christ. This is why we are reminded in Romans 8:1, *"There is no condemnation for those who belong to Christ Jesus."* The scripture then says that because we belong to Him, His Spirit has freed us from the power of sin. This means that once we repent, sin has no choice but to loose its constraining grip over our lives. Now all we have to do is forgive ourselves.

Today I encourage you to let go of past shortcomings. God has forgiven you and He doesn't even think about it, so stop trying to make Him recall. Let our prayer be, "God thank You for Your forgiving power that You offer me. Now help me to let go of my past and forgive myself. I want to operate in the liberty wherein You have given me through Jesus Christ."

Reflection Questions

1. What mistakes or bad decisions in your life have you struggled with forgiving yourself?
2. Why has forgiving yourself been such a hard task?
3. How different do you think the quality of your life would be if you forgave yourself and moved on?

Day 33
IT MAY HAVE BEEN YOUR DESIRE, BUT IT WASN'T YOUR DESTINY

Isaiah 55:8-11
> For my thoughts are not your thoughts, neither are your ways my ways, saith the Lord. For as the heavens are higher than the earth, so are my ways higher than your ways, and my thoughts than your thoughts. For as the rain cometh down, and the snow from heaven, and returneth not thither, but watereth the earth, and maketh it bring forth and bud, that it may give seed to the sower, and bread to the eater: So shall my word be that goeth forth out of my mouth: it shall not return unto me void, but it shall accomplish that which I please, and it shall prosper in the thing whereto I sent it.

When I was younger, my mother would always tell me, "Everything that glitters ain't gold." And the older I got, the more I understood her wise words. What she was saying to me was everything in life that appeals to me or that I may desire may not always be what is best for me.

Many times we plan out our lives. We plan our careers, future families, educational aspirations, social status, socio-economic status, and the list goes on and on. Unfortunately, more often than not, people subconsciously make these plans without first seeking God. We develop this enormous to-do list of life, but we never ask God if those desires are a part of His plan for our lives which is ultimately our destiny.

So as life begins to move forward, and our plans don't seem to work out the way we saw them, we get upset, discouraged, and sometimes even down right angry. But how can we feel disappointed when we didn't seek the Master's instructions?

God's thoughts and plans for our lives are far beyond anything that we could ever conjure up ourselves. Because He created us, we are His own masterpieces. He tailor makes each of us our own individualized path to our destiny. And when we start seeking or chasing after things that aren't on the path, God has no choice except to cause them to cease. He knows what's best.

So think about that relationship that failed. As much as you wanted it to work out, was it your destiny? Was the million dollar idea that crumbled before your eyes part of God's plan for your life? How about the job that you just knew was perfect and all of a sudden you had to walk away from it? Was it really your destiny to stay there?

When we attempt to move without God's guidance, we always end up lost. You can never go wrong seeking God's counsel and following His plan. It is always wise, precise, and will lead you to exactly where you are supposed to be.

So let our prayer be, "Lord, I don't want to make another move without You leading me. Show me how to pursue the life that You have destined for me to live. Let my thoughts and plans be Your thoughts and plans. Let my desires for my life line up with Your destiny for my life."

Reflection Questions

1. Think of a situation in your life that didn't work out the way you planned. What was your response?
2. Why do you think God's plans are so much more effective than your own?

Day 34

MOVING FROM EMOTIONAL TRIBULATION TO EMOTIONAL VICTORY

Luke 22:43
> Saying, Father if thou be willing, remove this cup from me: nevertheless not my will, but thine be done.

Because we are human, we have these tricky and sometimes deceptive feelings embedded in us called emotions. Our emotions make us feel happy, sad, fearful, excited and more. They are subject to change at any given time. God allows us to go through emotional tribulations to stir up our emotions. He allows this to happen to reveal to us our own emotional instability and gives us the opportunity to realize how much we need Him.

I understand that at times it can be difficult not being led by your emotions, but we must draw inspiration from Jesus, who exemplified putting His emotions at bay. According to the scripture, the night before Jesus died for us, He was in extreme emotional turmoil. He didn't want to die, this is why He said, *"If it be possible, remove this cup from me,"* but Jesus was able to move beyond His emotions and pray, *"Not my will, but thine will be done."* Jesus wasn't led by His emotions and neither should we. When God allows situations to affect us emotionally, we should seize the opportunity to step into a place of absolute trust. So instead of falling victim to our emotions, we should take authority over them and stay focused on the assignment, just like Jesus did.

So let our prayer be, "God thank You for the emotional trials that You allowed me to go through. Lord increase my faith so that I will trust You more to restore me to complete emotional wholeness. Thank you for my victory over my emotions and Your complete will being done in my life."

Reflection Questions

1. Have you ever battled against gaining control over your emotions? Explain.
2. What do you think will happen if you relinquish control of your emotions to God?

Day 35

THEY WILL FOLLOW YOUR EXAMPLE BEFORE THEY FOLLOW YOUR INSTRUCTION

I Timothy 4:11-16 (The Message)
> Get the word out. Teach all these things. And don't let anyone put you down because you're young. Teach believers with your life: by word, by demeanor, by love, by faith, by integrity. Stay at your post reading Scripture, giving counsel, teaching. And that special gift of ministry you were given when the leaders of the church laid hands on you and prayed—keep that dusted off and in use. Cultivate these things. Immerse yourself in them. The people will all see you mature right before their eyes! Keep a firm grasp on both your character and your teaching. Don't be diverted. Just keep at it. Both you and those who hear you will experience salvation.

In my profession of teaching, one thing I've learned about my students is that they are always looking to me as an example. They will do what I do before they do what I say. As a result of my own lack of discipline, getting to work on time is something that I often struggled with. Sometimes I would literally be running in before the bell rang. Now as inappropriate as that was, I would oftentimes fuss at my students for being late to class. I know! I know that is the pot calling the kettle black. But one day the Lord genuinely convicted me, not only concerning my own tardiness, but also because I was teaching one thing and living another.

I couldn't expect a specific behavior from my students if I myself was not willing to model it.

The same lesson is offered in this scripture. As Christians, we are representatives of Christ. Our lives should model His. Others should be able to see His love, His mercies, His grace, His compassion, His demeanor, and His character through us. We can't take the kingdoms of this world and make them the kingdoms of our Lord and Savior Jesus Christ if we aren't willing to live a lifestyle of excellence. This means we must show the world good character. We must show them integrity. We can't be liars and manipulators. We can't say one thing and do another. We must have a standard of righteous that we are unwilling to compromise. We will never influence the world if we won't come out of the world. Remember, non-believers are looking at you. Your actions can either draw them closer to or push them away from Christ. The more we expose the world to excellence and righteousness, the more they will model.

So let our prayer be, "Lord let my life reflect You in every way, shape, and form. When people see me, let them see You through me. Let my words, behaviors, and actions model You. Help me to be the best representation of You that I can."

Reflection Questions

1. What does your lifestyle portray Christ to look like?
2. Can you identify any areas in your life that you know there is room for you to better operate in excellence? If so, please explain.

Day 36

FROM A FAITH TALKER TO A FAITH WALKER: IS YOUR FAITH LIVING OR IS IT DEAD?

James 2:26
> For as the body is without the spirit is dead, so faith without works is dead also.

A verb is any word that represents an action. The word faith is defined as *confidence or trust in a person or a thing.* Now in order to trust someone or something, you must believe. All of these words – faith, trust, and believe – are all action words. This means that they all require you to do something.

If you go to school for years and learn a plethora of information, graduate, and never use or apply what you have learned, the knowledge is absolutely useless. Faith is the same way. If we scream to the top of our lungs day in and day out that we have faith in God and we believe His promises, but we don't spend time in His presence, develop a lifestyle of prayer, and won't sacrifice our own desires to do His work, our faith then becomes like that unused knowledge, USELESS.

God talk without God acts is outrageous nonsense. Faith and works are yoked partners. That means you can't have one without the other. Attempting to separate the two causes your faith to die.

Let's look at Abraham as an example. In Genesis 22, Abraham's faith was brought to life when he took Isaac to the mountain to be sacrificed. Even though Abraham talked a good faith talk, it wasn't until he got up and put some action to his belief that his faith gained power and authority. So as we move forward, let us be more like Abraham; let's put some work to our faith. Our prayer should be, "Lord help me to not only trust You more, but to be willing to do the work that my faith requires. Help me to be less of a faith talker and more of a faith walker."

Reflection Questions

1. What is something that you are currently believing and trusting God for?
2. What can you do to add some work to your faith?

Day 37

SHEDDING DEAD WEIGHT

Hebrews 12:1-2
> Wherefore seeing we also are compassed about with so great a cloud of witnesses, let us lay aside every weight, and the sin which doth so easily beset us, and let us run with patience the race that is set before us, Looking unto Jesus the author and finisher of our faith; who for the joy that was set before him endured the cross, despising the shame, and is set down at the right hand of the throne of God.

One of the most notable things about the high school where I teach is our track team. Our girls track team is nationally ranked and quite a few of the team members are nationally ranked as well. In a personal observation I see how intense the track team trains and prepares not just to win races, but to become better athletes. In conversation with one of the stars of the team, I took great notice to the uniform she was wearing. Upon my first look I thought to myself that she needed to put some clothes on; however, upon closer inspection I had somewhat of an epiphany.

In order to increase the speed and efficiency of their running, track stars understand that they don't need to have any extra weight. Their uniforms must be form fitted because if wind is able to get in, it could slow them down. They realize that their bodies must be extremely lean because the more bulky they are, the slower they will run.

So track stars come to the realization that in order to reach their goal which is to win the race, they must let go of anything that would weigh or slow them down. This same concept applies to us spiritually. God has promised us an expected end. He has promised us health, wealth, effective ministries, fulfilled dreams, new opportunities, and the ability to complete kingdom assignments. And if we ever plan to accomplish these things, we must let go of our extra weight.

My question to you today is what is it that is weighing you down? What is it that is holding you back from fully pursuing the promises of God without hesitation, delay, or reservation?

Let our prayer be, "God help me to shed any excess weight that is delaying me from fully pursuing You. God anything that would postpone or slow down my progress in chasing You, give me the strength, the courage, and the power to let it go!"

Reflection Questions

1. What is it that is weighing you down and preventing you from fully pursuing the promises of God for your life without any hesitation?
2. If you were to let go of those weights, what do you stand to gain?

Day 38
THE CHANGING OF THE SEASONS

Ecclesiastes 3:1-8 (NLT)
> For everything there is a season, a time for every activity under heaven. A time to be born and a time to die. A time to plant and a time to harvest. A time to kill and a time to heal. A time to tear down and a time to build up. A time to cry and a time to laugh. A time to grieve and a time to dance. A time to scatter stones and a time to gather stones. A time to embrace and a time to turn away. A time to search and a time to quit searching. A time to keep and a time to throw away. A time to tear and a time to mend. A time to be quiet and a time to speak. A time to love and a time to hate. A time for war and a time for peace.

Several years ago, the contemporary Gospel psalmist, Israel Houghton wrote and produced a song and the chorus stated:

It's a new season, it's a new day.
A fresh anointing is flowing my way.
It's a season of power and prosperity.
It's a new season coming to me.

A season is a *period of the year characterized by particular conditions of weather and temperature*. It is a time characterized by a particular circumstance or feature (it's cold and snowy in the winter, the leaves change colors in the fall, it's extremely rainy in the spring, and it's scorching hot in the summer). Most people who know me know that I really don't like winter. I hate being cold. I don't like snow, unless it's on my two free days that the Winston-Salem/Forsyth County School System says I don't have to make up. I don't like wearing layers of clothes. I'm not a fan of the sun going down at 5:00 pm, and it's just an overall dreary time of year for me.

However, whether I like it or not, winter has to come every single year! It doesn't matter if I approve, in December I can look forward to bone chilling, cold weather for the next three months. Now even though I don't like winter, many necessary things come from it. The snow that I despise kills the germs that cause so many people to battle sickness during the winter. That same snow cleans air so that when spring comes, we won't have so many people sneezing, coughing, and eyes watering. People will be able to breathe better and have a better quality of life because during the season that I dread so much, great works are being done.

This same scenario is often played out in our lives. Seasons change in our lives. As we grow, the Lord may begin to change our circle, our environment, or even our careers. He may begin to move people out of your life that you thought would be there forever. He may place new people in your life that you would have never thought of. And as uncomfortable as the changing of the season may be, just like with the four seasons of the year, they have to happen. Whether you like it or not, the seasons will and must change.

If the seasons don't change, you will have to deal with unnecessary crud, some unfortunate humps and bumps, delayed blessings, unwarranted hurts and pains (both physical and spiritual), and possibly some extreme misfortune. So instead of fighting, complaining, and wishing it away, embrace the changing of the seasons in your life. They are necessary! They have to happen! This new season is only making you better, stronger, purging out, putting in, and preparing you; so go with it!

Instead of wrestling with God about holding on to what He wants to remove in your life, let Him do His work. Let your prayer be, "God even though it's uncomfortable; even though it may hurt; and even if it comes in a manner in which I didn't expect, God change my seasons. Do it Your way, because You know what is best for me."

Reflection Questions

1. Have you been wrestling against God ordained changes in your life? If so, explain.
2. Why has this been something that you have fought against?
3. What setbacks could possibly occur as a result of not allowing God to change your season?

Day 39

DON'T SETTLE FOR AN ISHMAEL WHEN GOD PROMISED YOU AN ISAAC

Genesis 15:2-5 (The Message)
> Abram said, "GOD, Master, what use are your gifts as long as I'm childless and Eliezer of Damascus is going to inherit everything?" Abram continued, "See, you've given me no children, and now a mere house servant is going to get it all." Then GOD's Message came: "Don't worry, he won't be your heir; a son from your body will be your heir." Then he took him outside and said, "Look at the sky. Count the stars. Can you do it? Count your descendants! You're going to have a big family, Abram!"

In a few chapters of the book of Genesis, God promises Abram many things. But Abram asks God, "What good is all of these things if you aren't going to allow me to have children?" God responded to Abram, "If you can count the stars, then you will be able to count the number of children I will give you." Now even though God promised Abram this, he was extremely old. And as the years went by he still had no children.

So growing impatient because she had not been able to bear a child for Abram, his wife Sarai offered her servant Hagar to Abram to have him a child. Hagar bore a child and called his name Ishmael. As the scriptures continue, we learn that Sarai did eventually give Abraham a son and they called him Isaac. Isaac represents God's true promise.

So how does this apply to us? Time and again, God makes promises to us, and we, like Sarai, grow impatient waiting on God's promises to be fulfilled. Because of our impatience we make irrational decisions or act in disobedience which causes the Lord to be displeased. And although things may look good, it's not God's will being done in our lives. So today I encourage you to wait on the Lord. Stand firmly on His promises. Don't let your impatience cause you to settle for an Ishmael when God has promised you an Isaac.

Reflection Questions

1. Can you recall an area in your life that you have either settled or entertained the idea of settling? Explain.
2. What are the drawbacks of your decision to settle?
3. What benefits would come forth if you choose not to settle?

Day 40

GREAT THINGS START SMALL

Mark 30-34
> And he said, Whereunto shall we liken the kingdom of God? or with what comparison shall we compare it? It is like a grain of mustard seed, which, when it is sown in the earth, is less than all the seeds that be in the earth: But when it is sown, it groweth up, and becometh greater than all herbs, and shooteth out great branches; so that the fowls of the air may lodge under the shadow of it. And with many such parables spake he the word unto them, as they were able to hear it. But without a parable spake he not unto them: and when they were alone, he expounded all things to his disciples.

In this parable, Jesus is comparing His Kingdom to a mustard seed. The mustard seed is very small in size. To the natural eye it looks like nothing can be accomplished from it. However, when the mustard seed grows to full fruition, its size is grand. Its branches are big enough for birds to find shade under them. Who would have ever thought that something so small could become something so grandiose?

So how does this lesson relate to us? You may have thought of yourself as being small. You may have thought that you don't have much to offer. You may have thought your ideas were unimportant. You may have thought your gifts and talents were insignificant. You may have even thought that you were the most unlikely to do something great. In actuality, it is the complete opposite. God will bring forth a tremendous harvest if you yield to Him whatever it is you have, regardless of the size. Remember, God is always looking for a way to raise you up and use you for His glory. Size doesn't matter in His sight, only a willing heart is needed.

Who would have thought that a little girl born into poverty in the backwoods of Mississippi would grow up and become Oprah Winfrey? Can you imagine a homeless man living out of his car becoming Tyler Perry? What about a little boy from a single parent home ending up being President Barack Obama? What about stuttering Moses, lying Jacob, depressed Jeremiah, or cussing Peter? To the natural eye, all of these people appeared unlikely to become significant, but through Christ became great.

So as we move forward, remember it doesn't matter how small your beginnings appear, God can and will make you great in His sight. Your ideas aren't pointless; your innovations aren't purposeless; your creations aren't worthless; and your goals aren't unobtainable. God wants to grow your seeds into something amazing. So let our prayer be, "Lord thank You for all that You have placed inside of me. Thank You for cultivating the seeds in me. I know that even though I may not seem to have much to offer, You are growing me into something that the world needs and You can use. Thank You for my small beginnings."

Reflection Questions

1. What ideas, plans, and goals have you had that you may have felt were too small to ever come to pass?
2. Are you willing to yield those same ideas, plans, and goals to Christ so that He can bring them to fruition?

Day 41

A Closed Mouth Won't Get Fed

James 1:5 (The Message)
> If you don't know what you're doing, pray to the Father. He loves to help. You'll get His help, and won't be condescended to when you ask for it.

As a teacher, I always encourage my students to ask questions if there is something they don't understand. If there is a problem that they can't seem to figure out, they have free rein to ask for help. Now it behooves me when students know they don't understand a particular concept but they refuse to ask for assistance. Help is there; all they have to do is ask.

Many times we play out this same scenario when it comes to living for Christ. He understands that we don't have all the answers. That's not what He expects from us. Living in Christ is an on-going learning process. This is why James encourages us to ask for His help when we don't know what to do. When your back is up against the wall, all you have to do is ask for help. When you are in a situation and you can't seem to escape it, just ask for help. If there is a problem that you can't solve, help is there for you. All you have to do is ask. And when you ask for help, you don't have to worry about being ridiculed or chastised. As a matter of a fact, God takes pleasure in knowing that you are looking to Him for guidance and instruction. It is His desire that you turn to and seek Him when you don't know what to do. He wants to help you.

Understand that you have the Master Teacher right at your fingertips. There is no need to aimlessly wonder around trying to figure out how to navigate life alone. All you have to do is open your mouth and ask your God for instructions. He is waiting to answer all of your questions. So let your prayer be, "Lord, thank You for always being readily available to help me. Thank You for the opportunity to boldly come to You with any problem or issue that I may have. Thank You for not holding those things that I don't know against me. Thank You for your help!"

Reflection Questions

1. Can you think of situation or an issue that you are currently dealing with that you genuinely need God's help? Explain.
2. What has prevented you from asking for the help that you need?

Day 42

OPPORTUNITY IS KNOCKING

Jeremiah 29:11
> For I know the thoughts that I think toward you, saith the Lord, thoughts of peace, and not of evil, to give you an expected end.

"When opportunity came, it appeared in a different form and from a different direction than Barnes had expected. That is one of the tricks of opportunity. It has a sly habit of slipping in by the back door, and often it comes disguised in the form of any misfortune, or temporary defeat. Perhaps this is why so many fail to recognize opportunity."

-"Think and Grow Rich" by Napoleon Hill

Have you ever been in a situation where you prayed and prayed for God to give you an opportunity to be better, do better, or live better? In your mind did you see the opportunity? Did you convince yourself that you knew who and where the opportunity would come from? Occasionally, for some strange reason, we consciously and subconsciously tell God we know better than He does the plans for our lives. We may not necessarily say it out of our mouths, but our actions speak loud and clear. We tell Him how the opportunities should show up, what they should look like, and who should present them to us.

Then when our plans don't work out, we become disappointed or discouraged and sometimes even bring charges against God. When we do this, we only complicate and delay the doors that God is trying to open for us. So while we are sitting around trying to figure out why God didn't show up or come through, little do we know that God has already put into place a divine plan that is greater than any that we could ever imagine.

The quote from *Think and Grow Rich* reminds us that opportunity is subtle. It's not flashy, fancy or glamorous. It usually comes dressed in overalls. This means opportunity requires us to work. It causes us to have to get dirty. It causes us to have to fight for what is rightfully ours. So instead of fighting against opposition, grab hold to it. It is only opportunity in disguise.

Let our prayer be, "Lord thank You for the opportunities that You have presented before me. Help me to recognize them so that I won't fight against them. I know that Your thoughts and plans for my life are far greater than those that I have for myself, so the next time opportunity knocks, I will answer."

Reflection Questions

1. Are there any opportunities that you think you may have overlooked because they didn't appear in the manner wherein you thought they would?
2. What can you do now to take full advantage of the opportunities that are currently being presented to you?

Day 43

LORD HELP MY DISBELIEF

Mark 9:17-24

> And one of the multitude answered and said, Master, I have brought unto thee my son, which hath a dumb spirit; And wheresoever he taketh him, he teareth him: and he foameth, and gnasheth with his teeth, and pineth away: and I spake to thy disciples that they should cast him out; and they could not. He answereth him, and saith, O faithless generation, how long shall I be with you? how long shall I suffer you? bring him unto me. And they brought him unto him: and when he saw him, straightway the spirit tare him; and he fell on the ground, and wallowed foaming. And he asked his father, How long is it ago since this came unto him? And he said, Of a child. And ofttimes it hath cast him into the fire, and into the waters, to destroy him: but if thou canst do any thing, have compassion on us, and help us. Jesus said unto him, If thou canst believe, all things are possible to him that believeth. And straightway the father of the child cried out, and said with tears, Lord, I believe; help thou mine unbelief.

Earlier in the year, my church held its annual Ordination Service. The night before the service a pipe burst in the basement of the church, and the basement began to flood. There were a few of us who were there into the wee hours of the morning trying to figure out what to do and how to remove and dispose of this massive amount of water.

Now as I stood downstairs only a few feet away from the flood, the parable in this scripture came back to my remembrance. As I started to walk and clean and pray, I began to feel like the father in this scripture. Just like this father, I knew that God is the God of the impossible and that there is nothing that He cannot perform. Just like the father, my prayer then became Lord, help thou my unbelief! I asked God to help us to trust Him even the more to do what we know He is more than capable of doing.

So the next day came, the service was amazing, and God was glorified. How many of us have been or are in this place in our personal lives? We know who God is and we know what He is capable of doing, but for some reason, we allow ourselves to get anxious and worried or even fearful. When we are in the last hour – or as I like to call it, crunch time – we begin to doubt God and His ability.

I am simply here to encourage you to take on the mindset of the father. Let our prayer be, "Lord, I know that there is nothing that is impossible with You if I believe. So today I pray that You help me to trust and believe You even the more. God, the areas in my life that I struggle with trusting You, increase my faith in those places even the more. And help my unbelief!"

Reflection Questions

1. In what areas are you struggling to wholeheartedly trust God?
2. What is causing you to be anxious, worried, or even doubtful?
3. Can you think of a time where God did something in your life that you thought was impossible? Do you think He can do it again?

Day 44

DON'T LET YOUR FEELINGS MAKE YOU FORGET

Luke 17:11-19
> And it came to pass, as he went to Jerusalem, that he passed through the midst of Samaria and Galilee. And as he entered into a certain village, there met him ten men that were lepers, which stood afar off: And they lifted up their voices, and said, Jesus, Master, have mercy on us. And when he saw them, he said unto them, Go shew yourselves unto the priests. And it came to pass, that, as they went, they were cleansed. And one of them, when he saw that he was healed, turned back, and with a loud voice glorified God, And fell down on his face at his feet, giving him thanks: and he was a Samaritan. And Jesus answering said, Were there not ten cleansed? but where are the nine? There are not found that returned to give glory to God, save this stranger. And he said unto him, Arise, go thy way: thy faith hath made thee whole.

This scripture isn't new to most of us. Most of us know the story of the ten lepers. Ten men who'd been disease stricken for many years saw that Jesus was coming through their village and when He came, they began to cry out to Him for healing. Jesus gave them clear instruction and when they followed, they were instantly healed. The story continues that after the ten were healed, nine went on their merry way, but ONE came back.

The difference between the other nine and the one who came back is that the other nine allowed their newness, their wholeness, and their blessing to cause them to forget. They were no longer feeling desperate, unclean, or like an outcast; they were now healed, delivered and new!

How many times do we replay this same scenario in our own lives? We beg and plead God to heal our situation and He generously blesses us, but then we began ignore to Him after we receive what we want or need from Him. The nine that didn't come back became comfortable in their healing and didn't see as much of a need to cry out to or seek God anymore.

Do we do the same thing? God gives us the desire of our hearts and all of a sudden we don't pray, read our Bibles, fast or give like we once did when we needed God to work on our behalf. We don't seek God like we did when we were in despair. When we do this, this puts us in the same category with the nine who didn't come back to glorify Christ.

We must not get so comfortable in our "new" place that we do not continuously acknowledge and seek after Christ! The same zeal that we possessed for Christ and His will when we stood in need is the same zeal that we must keep after He blesses us.

So let our prayer be, "Lord thank You all of Your blessings. Help me not to become too comfortable in Your blessings. Help me to continuously be zealous in seeking You and Your will for my life. Help me not to forget!"

Reflection Questions

1. Have you become stagnant in your zeal for pursuing the things of Christ?
2. If so, why?
3. What can you do to rekindle your flame?

Day 45

FROM TRAGEDY TO TRIUMPH

Romans 5:3-4 (Amplified Version)
> Moreover [let us also be full of joy now!] let us exult and triumph in our troubles and rejoice in our sufferings, knowing that pressure and affliction and hardship produce patient and unswerving endurance. And endurance (fortitude) develops maturity of character (approved faith and tried integrity). And character [of this sort] produces [the habit of] joyful and confident hope of eternal salvation.

Last year a friend of mine transitioned from his earthly vessel and took his rightful place in heaven. During the celebration of life, the pastor made mention to the fact that the young man had rededicated his life back to Christ merely 48 hours before his passing. In the course of the service, I was able to bear witness to an awesome move of God that came through that church. The Holy Spirit moved and as a result, ten people accepted salvation and recommitted their lives back to Christ.

So as I sat there in awe of what God was doing, the Lord reminded me of His innate ability to turn tragedy into triumph! Tragedy is defined as an event causing great suffering, destruction, and distress, such as a serious accident, crime, or natural catastrophe. Triumph is the complete opposite. It is the act, fact, or condition of being victorious; the very happy or joyous feeling that comes from victory.

At a time set aside for grieving, mourning and fundamentally, a time of TRAGEDY for his family and friends, the spirit of the living God took hold of the service and right before my eyes, I was able to observe the victory that we always have in Christ. In a time that should have been set aside to recognize tragedy, the Lord moved and as those souls were saved and recommitted, the heavens rejoiced and the angels sang!

So my question to you is what tragic situation in your life is God waiting on you to let go of and give to Him so that He can show you what triumph and victory looks like? Allow the Lord to take you from tragedy to triumph!

Reflection Questions

1. What tragic situation in your life is God waiting on you to release to Him?
2. How do you think your story of tragedy to triumph can/will benefit others? Explain.

Day 46

SALT AND LIGHT

Matthew 5:13-16 (NLT)
> "You are the salt of the earth. But what good is salt if it has lost its flavor? Can you make it salty again? It will be thrown out and trampled underfoot as worthless. "You are the light of the world—like a city on a hilltop that cannot be hidden. No one lights a lamp and the puts it under a basket. Instead, a lamp is placed on a stand, where it gives light to everyone in the house. In the same way, let your good deeds shine out for all to see, so that everyone will praise your heavenly Father.

In my earlier teaching years, I always dreaded teaching ninth graders. On one hand, they were a little naive and a lot easier to mold into model high school students. But on the other hand, ninth graders went from being the top dogs of their school, Mr. or Miss Popular, and the big chief in June to being the babies in a place full of what seem to be adults and back to the bottom of the totem pole in August. So ninth graders are now trying to find their place to fit in. Some excel in academics; some find extracurricular activities to join; and others simply begin to display poor behavior and land in trouble. In a nutshell, ninth graders go through an identity crisis.

An identity crisis is a period of uncertainty and confusion in which a person's sense of identity becomes insecure, typically due to a change in their expected aims or role in society. With each new promotion, elevation, or stage of your life, you will find yourself asking the question, "Who am I?"

Just as I declare to my ninth graders, you also are a world changer, history maker, ground breaker, atmosphere changer, and foundation shaker. You are a peace keeper, effective leader, enlightened thinker, and standard raiser. You walk in great expectation because you know the God you serve is more than able to do exactly what you need Him to do. You are salt that adds the flavor of righteousness and light that guides and directs. You are not a follower, distraction, problem causer, or drama seeker.
So as you move into your next level in Christ, go with the mindset that you are a stalwart that God has called out to season your environment and to be a light that draws others to Christ.

Reflection Questions

1. Who are you? Describe yourself (highlighting your attributes) in a few sentences.
2. In what way do you think God is calling you out to be a standout?

Day 47

A Lesson From A Snowflake

Nehemiah 4:16-18 (NLT)
> But from then on, only half my men worked while the other half stood guard with spears, shields, bows, and coats of mail. The leaders stationed themselves behind the people of Judah who were building the wall. The laborers carried on their work with one hand supporting their load and one hand holding a weapon. All the builders had a sword belted to their side. The trumpeter stayed with me to sound the alarm.

During this past snow storm, I sat in my living room and watched as the snow began to fall. Upon observation, I noticed how delicate and fragile the snowflakes were. If they hadn't been falling so profusely, they would have been virtually unnoticeable. The longer I sat, the more snowflakes came. This thought came to my mind: individually, the snowflakes have no power. If they fell from the sky without the others, you would never even pay them any attention. However, when they all work together, what a beautiful masterpiece they become. When the snowflakes combine their efforts, they have the power make people stop, business come to a halt, clean the air, and make the environment better. Now imagine what the world would be like if we all took on the mindset of the snowflake.

This takes me back to the story told in Nehemiah. As the book opens, Nehemiah asks the king for permission to go to Jerusalem to rebuild the walls/gates that the enemies have torn down and burned. The king grants Nehemiah's request. Once in Jerusalem, Nehemiah inspects the walls and immediately commands the people to start rebuilding. Now the beautiful part of this story is that none of the people murmured, none of them complained. None of them came up with any excuses or took the lazy route. Everybody who could did. As the story continues, people came from all over to help rebuild this wall. The entire third chapter is dedicated to all those who came to help. The people were so committed to accomplishing the task, that in the fourth chapter, even when their enemies began to plot against them to stop their work, they developed a plan. They never stopped working. At all times of the day, men were working on the wall. With one hand they worked, and with the other hand they held their weapons. Eventually the wall was completely restored. But this could have never been accomplished if each individual did not do their part. Their minds were set on finishing the task at hand.

So how does this apply to us? What if everybody who could, would freely offer what we have. This would include our gifts, talents, time, energy, and efforts, to ensure the vision of your local assembly was executed. What would that look like? What if there were no excuses, no "I would, but," no "I can't," no "they can get somebody else," no "I don't feel like it," no "I'm tired," no "but what about my life," no "I don't want to be at church all the time, no nothing" And instead, just a few "what can I do to help," a couple of "I don't have much but what I do have I freely offer," a bit of "I really don't know how, but I'm willing to learn," and even a tinge of "whatever it takes, I'm willing to do's."

Just like the snowflakes, and the people in Jerusalem who rebuilt the wall, we work better when everybody is doing their part. The work doesn't become burdensome. The work becomes enjoyable and even fun. We create beautiful masterpieces when we all do it together! So let our prayer be, "Lord, what is it that I can do to make the vision and moreover the Kingdom, more effective and efficient? What areas can I offer more? How can I alleviate the burden? Lord what can I do to help?"

Reflection Questions

1. Can you think of areas in your life where you can offer more to the greater cause to make it more effective and efficient? If so, what are they?
2. What would happen if you completely threw yourself into something bigger than yourself, withholding nothing?

Day 48

ONE MAN'S TRASH IS ANOTHER MAN'S TREASURE

II Corinthians 5:17
> Therefore if any man be in Christ, he is a new creature: old things are passed away; behold, all things are become new.

Recycling is a process to change waste into new products in order to prevent the waste of potentially useful materials. When you look at trash, what do you think? Do you look at trash as something that is useless, dirty, and disgusting? Or do you look at trash as something that can be reused and if it lands in the hands of the right person, can be turned into something of great value.

Usually we knowingly and unknowingly view and treat other people the same way that we treat trash. We look at their past faults, past failures, and current situations and we make up in our own minds that they don't have anything of value to offer. However, trash is given a new purpose when it is recycled. What would happen if we gave people the opportunity to go through the recycling process? What would happen if we didn't focus on the faults and shortcomings (the trash) of others, and instead we saw the beauty and the recycling capabilities of what is inside of them?

God provided numerous examples throughout the Bible of people whom society had written off as trash, but were forgiven, cleaned up and reused to do mighty works. And if God, in all of His glory, can love, value, and use what was once useless, who are we not to offer that same type of compassion and opportunity to others? Remember, you were once "trash" according to "them," but to "Him" you were worth the cross.

So let our prayer be, "Lord help me to see the value in others that You see. Help me to focus on their treasure and not their trash."

Reflection Questions

1. Can you identify any part(s) of your life (problem, situation, issue, addiction, etc.) that was once trash but the Lord has turned into something useful (maybe a testimony)?
2. Have you ever been inspired by someone else's "recycled" testimony?
3. How can you use your past failures and mistakes help somebody else?

Day 49

YOU CAN'T ACCESS THE PROMISE WITHOUT FOLLOWING THE INSTRUCTION

Matthew 6:33 (NLT)
> Seek the Kingdom of God above all else, and live righteously, and he will give you everything you need.

After every lesson in my Civics class, my students usually take a quiz the following day. Since the beginning of the school year I always tell my students to go home and study their notes from that day. I tell them they should spend at least 20 minutes reviewing the lesson and mastering the vocabulary. My instruction to them is simple. If you take the time to study at home and not solely depend on the 10 minutes I give at the beginning of the next class, you will do well on the summary quiz.

Some students take heed to the instructions. They go home, study, make flash cards, and highlight specific vocabulary. When they come in the next morning, that 10 minute period I give those students simply skim through their notes because they know they are prepared. They aren't rattling through papers, trying to close their eyes and commit things to memory, looking like life is over, and saying Hail Mary's. These students have followed the instructions ensuring that they will receive a good grade!

This shows us that those who followed the instructions were able to receive the promise! Matthew 6:33 gives us this same lesson. In the beginning of the scripture, Jesus is offering the instruction. He is telling us to SEEK His kingdom above everything else. He is telling us to set our affections on Him – to seek His will, way, heart, instruction, chastisement and correction. He is instructing us to forsake ourselves, submit wholly to Christ, and honor Him in everything we do. He is instructing us to live right, do good, have integrity, and operate in excellence.

And then here comes the promise in the latter part of the verse. It says He will give us everything we need! This everything includes fullness, wholeness, physical and emotional healing, deliverance, financial breakthroughs, forgiveness, increase in faith, peace, joy, and anything else that we may be standing in the need of!

So let us move forward in following the instructions of God so that we can freely walk into and flourish in the promises of God!

Reflection Questions

1. Have you struggled either now or in the past in following God's precise instructions?
2. Why do you think it has been a struggle for you?

Day 50

FOOTPRINTS VERSUS FOSSILS

II Kings 23:25 (NLT)
> Never before had there been a king like Josiah, who turned to the Lord with all his heart and soul and strength, obeying all the laws of Moses. And there has never been a king like him since.

The late great Nelson Mandela said, "There's is no passion to be found playing small – in settling for a life that is less than the one you are capable of living."

We always hear about leaving your "footprint" in the sand. This statement refers to a person leaving their mark on some place or something, so that people will know they were there. Today I want to encourage you to leave more than a footprint, but a fossil in your lifetime.

A footprint is an impression left behind a person or an animal walking or running. You see, a footprint can be covered up, washed away, trampled over and soon forgotten. Now a fossil on the other hand is also an impression or a remnant of an object that was walking or running. The difference between the two is that a fossil has been preserved. A fossil can be covered up, tossed around, buried under dirt, and endure various extreme weather conditions, however, when it's all said and done, the fossil still has just as much impact and authenticity as it did the first day the creature stepped in that place.

In your own time, I encourage you to read the entire story of Josiah, which is found in 2 Kings 22-23. Josiah's reign as King began when he was 8 years old. He came from a lineage of kings who had turned away from God; however, as a child Josiah did what was right in the eyes of the Lord. He eventually renewed the covenant between God and the people. He ordered that all images created to worship the pagan gods in the temple be burned. He desecrated anything that did not bring glory to the true and living God. He got rid of the mediums and spiritualist. He made the people celebrate the Passover. And it was because of all of these things that the writer could say "Never before had there been a king like Josiah and there had never been a king like him. Josiah left his fossil in history.

So what world changing, life altering fossil is down inside of you, waiting to be left? What will you do in your lifetime that people will say there was never a (_____) like you before and there never will be again? What legacy will you leave? Will you leave a footprint or a fossil?

Reflection Questions

1. What ideas, inventions, or creations (fossils) are inside of you waiting to be brought to fruition?
2. What legacy do you plan to leave when you are gone?

Day 51

DON'T LET THE FIRE DIE
(STIR UP THE GIFTS)

II Timothy 1:6 (Amplified)
> That is why I would remind you to stir up (rekindle the embers of, fan the flame of, and keep burning) the [gracious] gift of God, [the inner fire] that is in you by means of the laying on of my hands [with those of the elders at your ordination].

In this scripture, Paul understands very clearly that Timothy has a gift that has not come into full bloom yet. He recognizes that his gifts can only be developed through being used. This is why he commands Timothy to stir up the gift.

There are gifts in you that have to be stirred up or used. There are people that are waiting on you and your gifts. Their lives are depending on what is inside of you. You are the gasoline that someone needs to ignite the engine to their destiny. If you don't allow God to use what He has placed inside of you, that person(s) will remain stagnated, going absolutely nowhere.

Don't allow the enemy to trick and deceive you into being selfish and robbing the Kingdom of God. If you are not allowing God to freely use your gifting, talents, and skills, then yes, you are a thief and a robber. It is a harsh reality, but it is the truth.

My assignment today is simple, just as Paul said to Timothy, I say to you, "Stir up the gifts!" Those things that are inside of you that the world needs, I speak life to them. I call them forward. I command you to operate in them. Today, make a sound decision not to let the flame die. Don't let those gifts go to waste. Don't leave others high and dry waiting on you. Don't cause someone else to miss out because you won't use what is inside of you.

You have so much in you to offer and the world is waiting. So let your prayer be, "God stir up and rekindle whatever it is inside of me that You placed in me to use. Lord completely remove me out of the way so that I will not hinder Your work in me. I refuse to rob your Kingdom. Lord, don't let the fire die."

Reflection Questions

1. What gifts are inside of you that need to be stirred up?
2. Have you held up the process of those gifts being stirred up? If so, how?
3. What do you think your gifts have to offer the Body of Christ?

Day 52

NO SHORTCUTS; YOU WILL MISS OUT ON THE JOURNEY

John 14:5-7 (NLT)
> "And you know the way to where I am going." "No, we don't know, Lord," Thomas said. "We have no idea where you are going, so how can we know the way?" Jesus told him, "I am the way, the truth, and the life. No one can come to the Father except through me. If you had really known me, you would know who my Father is. From now on, you do know him and have seen him!"

Periodically people ask me what benefits came from pledging my sorority. My response is simple. Pledging my sorority instilled in me life-long character building lessons that I will never forget. In 2005 as I pledged my sorority, I remember my big sisters telling me and my line sisters not to walk on the grass. Now I never understood exactly why I couldn't walk on the grass, but I did as I was told. It wasn't until the night before I officially became a member that my big sisters revealed the lesson in not walking on the grass. One of my sisters looked me straight in the eyes and told me that we couldn't walk through the grass because there were no shortcuts in life. Anything worth having in life was worth the journey that it would take to get to it. Her words continuously resound in my head. To this day I still do not walk on the grass.

In essence, this is the same lesson that Jesus is teaching the disciples in the scripture. As Jesus was preparing the disciples for His departure, Thomas asked Jesus, "How can we know the way?" Jesus reminded the disciples that He was "the way, the truth, and the life." He also told them that no one would be able to get to the Father unless they came through Him. There is no way above Him, no way under Him, no way around Him, but only through Him could the disciples have access to the Father.

The same lesson is still applicable to us today. The only way that we will gain entrance to the Father is through the doorway of Jesus. Religious antics won't get us there. Theological verbiage can't do it. Good deeds alone won't help. Piousness will push us away. Knowing all the church isms and jargon won't cut it.

The only way to the Father is to unconditionally love what He loves, and that is people. To get to know Him we must die to self. To gain access we have to be obedient to His will and His way. If we are going to meet Him we must live righteously. Simply put, there are no shortcuts! Shortcuts may appear easier, look like less work, or even seem more glorious, but we know the truth.

So as we move forward, let our prayer be, "Lord thank You for reminding me that there are no shortcuts to Your glory. Thank You for giving me the strength, the courage, and the endurance to take the journey. I know that even though the shortcuts seem easier, Your rewards are much greater than any shortcut I could ever take."

Reflection Questions

1. Are there any areas in your life that you have opted to take the shortcut instead of embracing the journey?
2. How do you think not taking the journey and missing out on the lessons that are offered will impact your life?

Day 53

KEEP YOUR EYES ON THE PRIZE

Philippians 3:13-14
> Brethren, I count not myself to have apprehended: but this one thing I do, forgetting those things which are behind, and reaching forth unto those things which are before, I press toward the mark for the prize of the high calling of God in Christ Jesus.

God has a specific plan for each of our lives. It is His desire that each and every one of us will eventually fulfill that plan. In this scripture, Paul lets us know that in order for us to fulfill that plan or reach the goal, we must first forget or let go of what is behind us. This means forgetting any past failures, hurts, wrong decisions, disappointments, mistakes, insecurities, unforgiveness, anger, and anything else that would attempt to hold us in the place where we used to be. We have to let those things go!

Those things that we need to let go of aren't only the "bad" things of our past. This also speaks to past accomplishments, our past achievements, our past accolades, and even our past victories. That's not saying that we should not bless God for the things He had already done, but we can no longer ride on those things. Yesterday's manna does us no good today.

One definition of the word press means to demand immediate attention or to give urgency to something. So how can we PRESS? We press by praying. We press by seeking God's face. We press by spending time in His presence. We press by studying His word. We press by chasing His glory. And our prize is being in and doing the will of our Father.

So as we move forward, let us take on the attitude of the author in Hebrews 12:1 and let go of every dead weight – especially our past – that would attempt to hold us in a place wherein we will not be able to reach our mark. I dare you to move forward and keep your eyes on the prize.

Reflection Questions

1. Is there anything in your life that you have struggled to "forget?"
2. Why has letting those things go proven to be so difficult?
3. What does your "press" look like? What can you do to move forward?

Day 54

SURPRISE OR NOT?

Jeremiah 1:5 (The Message)
> "Before I shaped you in the womb, I knew all about you. Before you saw the light of day, I had holy plans for you: A prophet to the nations— that's what I had in mind for you."

For some reason we sometimes think that we are a disappointment or letdown to God. We think that our actions, behavior and even our disobedience grieves God so much that He no longer wants to have anything to do with us. We may act as if He no longer believes in us or loves us. However, this is not true. In Jeremiah 1:5, God reminds Jeremiah that even before we were formed in our mother's womb, God already knew us! This means that He already knew every mistake, failure, bad decision, slip up and misfortune. Even though He knew all of this about us, He still doesn't change His mind about us!

God knows all of the unsavory situations that we will get ourselves into, but He is not surprised. Those things don't catch Him off guard! His love for us has already covered all of that. Remember 1 Peter 4:8 says, *"Most important of all, continue to show deep love for each other, for love covers a multitude of sins."*

So remember when you mess up, love is saying, "I got that!" When you fall down, love says, "I got that too!" When you stray left, love says, "That's covered!" When you fall by the wayside, love says, "Oh, that's nothing!"

When you get tripped up on the small things, love says, "That was already in the plan!"

Because God is our Father, nothing we do can ever make Him stop loving us. Our lives can never pull a "gotcha" on God because He always will look back at us and say, "No, I got you!" So let our prayer be, "God thank You for allowing Your love to always cover me! Thank You for never changing Your mind about me. I'm so grateful that because You created me, my life and mistakes never catch you by surprise."

Reflection Questions

1. Have you ever felt like you did something to let God down? Explain.
2. Do you believe that His love covers what you thought was a disappointment to Him?
3. How can you apply the principle in the above question to your life?

Day 55

HIS YOKE IS EASY

Matthew 11:28-30
> Come unto me, all ye that labour and are heavy laden, and I will give you rest. Take my yoke upon you, and learn of me; for I am meek and lowly in heart: and ye shall find rest unto your souls. For my yoke is easy, and my burden is light.

About mid way through the year during 2013, a friend of mine called me with some disturbing news. She informed me that her best friend's oldest son had been diagnosed with Hodgkin's Lymphoma and would immediately begin chemotherapy and radiation treatments. Her request was simple. She said, "India, I know you know how to pray, so please just pray!" So without delay, I began to pray. My prayers were precise and fervent. Not only did I pray for healing and wholeness, but I also prayed that God would give his mother strength to endure, peace for her spirit, and faith to move mountains! I prayed that God would draw her, her husband, and their 5 boys closer to Him even the more.

I started following her son's journey via a social media network and would encourage her and her husband anytime I was led. She and I eventually developed a relationship of our own.

On January 24, 2014 I logged on to a social media site and saw a picture that the mother posted. The picture was of the oldest son with the biggest smile on his face holding a sign that said, "Jameer is now Hodgkin's Lymphoma Free! Bye-bye cancer!" I immediately began to rejoice and thank God for His mighty works that He'd done in that little boy's life. I then sent a text to his mother letting her know how excited I was. As we texted back and forth this was one of her responses: "I can't thank you enough for your prayers. They have meant more than you know. We had no choice but to pray and leave it in God's hands. We knew Jameer would be healed and after a while, it was easy."

My thoughts instantly went to Matthew 11:28-30. A yoke is a frame fitted to a person's shoulders to carry a load in two equal proportions. Generally, you will see two animals joined at their heads by a yoke so that they can plow or pull a heavy load.

In this scripture, Jesus is giving very distinct instruction. Just like the young lady in the story, if you are tired, if you've been carrying around something, trying to figure out something, or trying to fix something, Jesus is bidding you to come and lay down and give your burden to Him. His desire for us is always to rest in Him. He tells us to take His yoke and learn from it. His yoke is easy. This means that the yoke that Christ offers us is not heavy, pressing, or hard. Instead it is useful, good, gracious, and it is pleasant! And because we have Christ in us, He makes our loads light to bare.

So my question to you is, "What burdens are you carrying around? What concerns in your life have you been trying to handle but keep coming up short? What issues do you have that God has been trying to take off of your plate? Today

I encourage you to give Him your "stuff." Let Him carry your burdens. He is far more equipped then you could ever be. Like the young mother, when you give your problems, issues, and stuff to Christ, it instantly becomes easy!

Reflection Questions

1. What cares in your life have you been trying to handle, but you keep coming up short?
2. Would it be more beneficial for you to continue trying to handle these situations or to relinquish them to God and allow Him to handle them for you? Explain your answer.

156

Day 56

WHAT'S ON YOUR MIND?

Philippians 4:8 (NLT)
> And now, dear brothers and sisters, one final thing. Fix your thoughts on what is true, and honorable, and right, and pure, and lovely, and admirable. Think about things that are excellent and worthy of praise.

Ancient Chinese poet Lao Tzu stated:
> "Watch your thoughts; they become words.
> Watch your words; they become actions.
> Watch your actions; they become habit.
> Watch your habits; they become character.
> Watch your character; it becomes your destiny."

A thought, in the context of a verb, is to consider for evaluation or for possible action upon. In his quote, Lao Tzu solidifies the power that our thoughts have. It has been proven that whatever we commit our thought processes to are the things that will be reflected in our words, actions, habits, and most importantly our character. This is why Paul reminds us of what we should fix our minds on.

We have the power to bring our thoughts under the submission of Christ. How do we do that? I'm glad you asked. Every time thoughts of fear try to creep in your mind think on God's truth that fear is merely false evidence appearing real. If worry or doubt peeps its head out, think about God's innate ability to do the impossible. When thoughts of lack seep into your brain think on God's promise to be provision. When feelings of loneliness try to trespass in your mind, think about how God told you that He would never leave you nor forsake you. These are the things that you know to be true. These are the things that you know to be right. These are things that are excellent and deserve your thoughts.

Your thoughts will dictate where your destiny will take you. So let our prayer be, "Lord take control of my thoughts. Guard my mind with Your salvation. Help me to only think on the things that bring You glory and praise. Fix my mind on You."

Reflection Questions

1. What thoughts have you allowed your mind to stay fixed on that you know do not match your destiny?
2. How can you counteract those same thoughts to match your destiny?

Day 57

THE MAN IN THE MIRROR

Psalm 139:23-24
> Search me, O God, and know my heart: try me, and know my thoughts: And see if there be any wicked way in me, and lead me in the way everlasting.

I've come to realize that it is much easier to point out the faults and shortcomings of others, rather than myself. It doesn't take much effort to nitpick the "defects" in my brothers and sisters. It's easy because subconsciously we look for error in others. We look for a "blame" person in case something doesn't work out or if a plan fails.

However, I love the approach that David took in the last few verses of this Psalm. Instead of placing blame on another person, instead of pointing a finger at someone else, his request was for God to search him (David). His desire was for God to show him those unpleasant and offensive characteristics about himself. You know those things that he probably didn't talk about often, and those things that he probably tried to hide from most people. I'm sure they included the struggles that he was ashamed to admit he had and those feelings that he attempted to bring under submission but just wouldn't seem to go away. Even more so, if David was anything like us, he also had thoughts that he didn't want to think, but he couldn't help thinking. All of those "things" caused David to pray this prayer.

When was the last time you prayed this same prayer? When was the last time you asked God to show you yourself? When was the last time you didn't pray for God to change another person, but simply to change you? Understand this is an issue that most people struggle with at one point or another in their lives. However, it is not something that most people desire to share with others. Most people don't prefer to share that there are some issues, habits, addictions, and thoughts that they are dealing with.

It is easier and more comfortable to deflect attention to another person's faults than to stand up to that person in the mirror. It takes guts to reflect on your own life and to call yourself out on your own mess. It takes courage to come clean that there may be some jealousy or some envy in your heart. It takes boldness to admit that you have held on to some unforgiveness. It takes tenacity to concede that haughtiness or pride creeps around your door occasionally. But if the truth be told, the sooner you allow God to deal with you on those secret issues, the sooner you will be able to move forward in truth and in pursuing the things God has called you to.

So let our prayer be, "God show me myself. Deal with me. Before I point out another error in someone else, reveal to me those things in my heart that are not pleasing to You and give me the strength and courage to let You change me. Show me the man or woman in the mirror!"

Reflection Questions

1. Do you find it easier to point out error in others than yourself? If the answer is yes, why do you think this is so?
2. When was the last time you asked the Lord to show you those things in you that don't please Him?
3. What benefits do you think will come from you allowing God to deal with the secret issues in your heart?

Day 58

IT WAS A SETUP!

Romans 8:28-30 (NLT)
> And we know that God causes everything to work together for the good of those who love God and are called according to his purpose for them. For God knew his people in advance, and he chose them to become like his Son, so that his Son would be the firstborn among many brothers and sisters. And having chosen them, he called them to come to him. And having called them, he gave them right standing with himself. And having given them right standing, he gave them his glory.

A while back, I began to playback the "film" of my life. I laughed about the great times, I took pride in the high times, I got teary-eyed concerning the hard times, and I rejoiced over the victorious times. My first semester teaching, I was given the task of teaching all 9th graders. I know, poor me! During that time my school put together a team for the Susan G. Komen "Race for the Cure" breast cancer walk. I began having conversations with my students, trying to encourage them to participate. During one class, I asked my students if they themselves or if they knew anyone who'd been affected by breast cancer. One young lady raised her hand. She shared that her mother was currently battling breast cancer. She told us that she wanted to participate in the walk, but she didn't have the money. Of course I paid the fee for her to participate and she had an amazing time!

Now during my second year teaching, I had another opportunity to teach this same young lady in another class. In that same school year, her mother lost her battle to cancer and passed away. Having lost my mother a few years prior, this was a soft spot for me. So I went to her home after the funeral and something in my spirit connected with hers. That day I made a commitment to God, the young lady, and her grandfather, who was raising her, that as long as I had breath in my body, I would be an active part of her life. In December of that same year, her father passed away. Her life instantly became a mirror image of my own. It wasn't until that moment that I understood I had to lose my parents 16 months apart so that I could effectively and authentically minister to this young lady. Her presence in my life answered so many "why me's" that had plagued me for years. If for no other reason, I had to go through that traumatic experience for her. Little did I know when my father transitioned to glory in June of 2002 and then when my mother transitioned in October 2003, that God would use my pain, victory and testimony to carry this young lady through. It was all a setup for that appointed time.

God has a plan for each of our lives. The experiences that we go through, especially the not so agreeable and wholesome ones, are all a part of His setup for our lives. Nothing we go through is just happenstance. God allows it, because He knows that there will come a time where He will use our pains, sorrows, and low times. He has a plan that will cause all of our hard times to work for our good.

So as we go through this week, think about the low points in your life wherein you question and asked why me? Now think on how God has already and is still taking those same issues and using them for your good and His glory. Remember, it was all a set up!

Reflection Questions

1. Have you ever had a "why me" moment? If so, describe that moment.
2. How did or can God eventually use that situation to help you or someone else?

Day 59

Please Don't Let Me Fall

Jude 1:24-25 (NLT)
> Now all glory to God, who is able to keep you from falling away and will bring you with great joy into His glorious presence without a single fault. All glory to Him alone is God, our Savior through Jesus Christ our Lord. All glory, majesty, power, and authority are His before all time, and in the present, and beyond all time! Amen.

Not too long ago, I found myself in an extremely low place, a place I had allowed myself to get to and had stayed entirely too long. As I lay in the middle of my friend's bedroom floor crying, weeping, and wailing, I felt my spirit falling, literally. I felt myself sinking deeper and deeper into a place that I was not physically or spiritually prepared to be. Through my uncontrollable tears, the only thing I could muster out was, "Jesus HELP!" And that is exactly what He did, He sent the Holy Spirit to help! Just before I hit the bottom that night, I felt the Holy Spirit catch me. And not only did He catch me, He reminded me of who He was and His power and authority that He possesses and that He has given me.

Now I've been in church my entire life and I've heard this scripture many times over as benedictions were given, but this night, this scripture came to life for me. To fall means to drop or descend under the force of gravity, as to a lower place through loss or lack of support. Another entity defines a fall as to leave an upright position suddenly and involuntarily. The scripture reminds us that God is able to prevent us from leaving that upright position where He has placed us in. Through Him, there is no lack of support that would even cause us to fall in the first place.

Not only does God prevent us from falling away from Him, but He renders us perfect, without fault in His presence. And He is excited and glad to do it. How amazing is that? From a place of uncertainty where you were about to lose everything – and a position in which you were hopeless, destitute, lonely, ready to give up, about to throw in the towel, or even let go – to being perfect in the sight of the true and living God! The same way He came to my rescue that night, He desires to rescue you too.

So my question to you is simple. Can you trust God enough to keep you from falling? Do you believe that He has all power and authority? Do you understand that there is no place that you could ever be where you are out of His reach? Let your prayer be, "God thank You for Your keeping power. Thank You for not only preventing me from falling, but catching me when I slip. I believe that You can rescue me from any situation that I willingly or unwillingly get into. Thank you for not letting me fall"

Reflection Questions

1. Can you recall a time in your life where God kept you from falling?
2. Do you understand that there is no place that you could ever be where you are out of His reach?

Day 60

IT WILL COST YOU EVERYTHING

Philippians 3:7-10
> But what things were gain to me, those I counted loss for Christ. Yea doubtless, and I count all things but loss for the Excellency of the knowledge of Christ Jesus my Lord: for whom I have suffered the loss of all things. And do count them but dung, that I may win Christ, and be found in Him, not having mine own righteousness, which is of the law, but that which is through the faith, the righteousness which is of God by faith: That I may know Him, and the power of His resurrection, and the fellowship of His suffering, being made conformable unto His death:

On January 1, 2013 I was in New Year's Watch Night Service at my church. I remember my Pastor making an appeal for those who were really ready to surrender to Christ to come down to the altar. Interestingly enough, total surrender had been pressing on my heart for some time now. I knew that I couldn't let this moment slip away. So I made my way to the altar and I had a life changing experience. That night I cried out to God (both figuratively and literally) and offered the sincerest YES that I could give. Now I've said yes before, but this time it was different. This yes was genuine. It was authentic. It was ready to go to work.

Little did I know, this YES was going to cost me everything, and I mean EVERYTHING! That yes cost me some relationships that I thought would be around forever. It cost me some unforgiveness that I'd been holding onto for years. It cost me some fears that had crippled me for far too long. It cost me some pride, the subtle kind. It cost me my ego. It cost me the option of living life on my own terms. It ultimately cost me my life.

But my gain was so much greater! I gained the opportunity to know Christ. Not just know Him by what I read or hear about Him, but I get to experience Him. I get to watch Him transform my life. I now have a consistent, continuous relationship with Christ that I am confident will never change. I've been made right through Him.

This experience is an excellent example of what Paul is eluding to in the scripture. When you say yes to Christ, there will be some things that you hold dear to you, some things that you think are profitable to you, that you will simply have to take as a lost. However in comparison to what will be cultivated in you and what will be done through you, what you are giving up is a life that is worthless and vile. Christ wants you to share in and receive the great benefit of His sufferings and of His resurrection.

So I am simply encouraging you to let go of everything! Be willing to give it all up for the sake of Christ. Whatever He is desiring of you to let go of, walk away from, jump ship on, cut off, lay down, and get rid of, do it today. He would never require you to let go of something if He didn't have something much better waiting for you. So let your prayer be, "God, whatever it is that I need to severe ties with in order to know and experience You more, give me the strength to do so. As much as I want to hold on, I am willing to pay whatever the cost may be to have more of You!"

Reflection Questions

1. What do you think a genuine "YES" to God will cost you?
2. Are you willing to let go of those things?
3. What do you think the benefit to your life will be if you forsake yourself and wholeheartedly submit to Him?

About the Author

Tenacious. Determined. Strong. Tough. Just as these attributes apply to Watty Piper's The Little Engine that Could, these are also characteristics used to describe India N. Reaves. Having faced many obstacles in life, she has an incomparable will to keep pressing and moving through any situation. Actively involved in educational, mentoring, political, community affairs, and religious pursuits, I'm T.O.U.G.H. is a logical extension of the weekly impartation called Solomon's Corner that is presented at Great Commission Community Church, Inc. where she is a Minister in Training. I'm T.O.U.G.H. is India's literary debut. We can't wait to see what she crafts next!

MORE PRAISE FOR I'M T.O.U.G.H.

"Whether you are new in the body of Christ or whether you have been a part of the body for years, the author's words are inspirational and thought-provoking. She reminds me that God is able no matter the obstacle I face. Whatever promise or dream God has implanted within my heart, it will flourish. A delay is not a denial!"
-Saprina Brown Taylor, Attorney

I found the reflections to be thought provoking and encouraging. The use of scripture and real life situations allow for practical application. I felt inspired to reconsider how my life is moving forward when I read the reflections provided.
-Katrina Y. Billingsley, Therapist

India would love to speak at your next event. She is also available for conferences, book signings and tours. To learn more and contact India, visit www.imtoughdevotional.com.